God, Self and Salvation in a Buddhist Context

God, Self and Salvation in a Buddhist Context

Rory Mackenzie

Copyright © 2014–2016 Rory Mackenzie

Published in 2017 by Wide Margin,
90 Sandyleaze, Gloucester, GL2 0PX, UK
http://www.wide-margin.co.uk/

The right of Rory Mackenzie to be identified as the Author of this Work has been asserted by him in accordance with the Copyright, Designs and Patents Act 1988.

All rights reserved. No part of this publication may be reproduced, stored in a retrieval system, or transmitted in any form or by any means electronic, or mechanical, photocopying, recording or otherwise, without the prior permission of the publisher or a licence permitting restricted copying.

ISBN 978-1-908860-19-4

Printed and bound in Great Britain by Lightning Source, Milton Keynes

For my parents Rod and Barbara:

With grateful thanks for all of their prayers, loyalty and generosity, not just to me but also to my wife Rosalyn and our three daughters.

Although no longer with us, fond memories and their many examples of selfless living live on.

Acknowledgements

There are a number of people who have read and commented on draft forms of this book. I appreciate the critical but helpful comments from two anonymous readers from the William Carey Library. Jim Pym lent me some useful material and made some interesting remarks on Pure Land Buddhism. Bob Trelogan, who has spent 37 years as a missionary in Central Thailand, made useful remarks on the manuscript. Professor Geoff Hunt read my chapter on 'Self' and made a number of helpful suggestions.

Dr John Jeacock produced a couple of diagrams for the book and was always on hand when I had 'computer problems', as was Andrew Dunipace. Some of this book was written during study leave from the International Christian College (now the Scottish School of Christian Mission) in Glasgow and I appreciate the research time that was made available to me.

Simon Cozens at Wide Margin has been a pleasure to work with. I have found his 'can do' attitude so refreshing, and I would like to thank him for his perceptive work on the text.

Last of all, a huge thank you to my wife and fellow traveller Rosalyn for her friendship, continuous support and yes, patience! She read drafts of my work, picking up on grammatical mistakes, and potential ambiguous statements.

Introduction

This book engages with a number of Buddhist beliefs and, where possible, uses them to explain aspects of God, self and salvation. I would like to think that a Buddhist who picks up this book will feel that I have demonstrated respect for his or her tradition and not colonized it in any way. Indeed, I hope that these chapters will cast some light on the Christian faith for Buddhists and other spiritual seekers.

Primarily though, this is a book for Christians who wish to develop their understanding of Buddhism. It may be that you are a missionary in Asia, or it could be that you live in the West, where there is a significant Buddhist diaspora and a considerable interest in Buddhism by westerners—as demonstrated, for example, through the rise of mindfulness. I appreciate that many effective missionaries take the view that an in-depth knowledge of Buddhism is *not* necessary to reach out to the Buddhist world. They have a point, and we should not wait until we have a deep understanding of the religious other before we reach out. That said, I take the view that as we try to understand the Buddhist worldview and reflect on the Christian Scriptures, we discover helpful ways of framing God's story. Indeed, any attempt to understand a religion on its own terms will normally draw us into friendships with people of that particular faith. This, in itself, is an enriching learning experience.

At the end of each chapter, there is an invitation to engage with some questions. This is intended to help you review the material and apply it to practice. If you do not want to start at the beginning, then start where you wish, as the chapters are reasonably self-contained. That said, an initial look at the appendix will provide you with an overview of Buddhist paths to liberation/enlightenment; this may provide a useful background for reading the book.

The first chapter examines the life and work of Norwegian missionary Karl Reichelt (1877-1952). I have drawn out five lessons which I have learnt from a study of Reichelt's ministry, and which I constantly try to apply to my own practice. These are:

- Keep Christ at the centre of all of life and ministry.

- Live in missionary encounter with others.

- Take a contextual approach despite the risks of being misunderstood.

- Study hard to understand the religious world of those I try to reach.

- Form and sustain genuine friendships.

The second chapter gives a brief overview of the cultural and religious milieu into which Gotama, the Buddha-to-be, was born. It then looks at the life of the Buddha through 12 acts, or 12 significant stages which, according to Buddhist teaching, every Buddha goes through. These acts function as a helpful paradigm around which to organise the life of the Buddha. The chapter then goes on to set out 12 aspects of Christ's ministry starting with his eternal existence to his return to our world at some future point.

The third chapter looks at why the Buddha did not discover God and the validity of the claim that some Christians make when they identify Jesus Christ as the next Buddha of our world (Maitreya). What are biblical attitudes to those of other faiths, particularly when religious images are involved? The chapter goes on to examines Paul's response to the plethora of religious images in Athens and how he engaged with different people in the synagogue, market place (*agora*) and the city fathers on Mars Hill. Paul was able to adjust his approach to monotheists, people from primal religious fraternities, those with the latest ideas, and then the gate keepers of the multi-faceted religious practices of the city of Athens.

The Old Testament prophet Jeremiah strikes me as being regretful at the presence of idols. Clearly, he longs for the day when people will recognise the emptiness of their inherited religious tradition and find in God what they could not find in their gods. The chapter concludes with a consideration of Abraham, who shows deep concern for the people of Sodom. God encourages Abraham to enter into a conversation with him. In that conversation with God, Abraham expresses concern for the people of Sodom in what is arguably the first example of intercessory prayer in the Christian Scriptures.

The fourth chapter asks to what extent we may compare God to the Buddhist *Dhamma*. Could this at least be a starting point for conversations with Buddhists? The question is important and my answer engages with some of the creative writing of the Thai scholar monk Venerable Buddhadasa (1906-1993). We consider what we mean by 'personal' when we talk about God and look at some ideas put forward by Hans Küng who suggests that when speaking of God, 'transpersonal' may be a more readily acceptable term for Buddhists than 'personal'. We also think about other Buddhist terms we might use to relate to God. It may well be that, for Tibetan Buddhists, it is more meaningful to start off a conversation by comparing God to the Primordial Buddha or the Ādi Buddha. Any comparison between God and the *Dhamma* is a penultimate rather than an ultimate idea, but it may be a place where we can begin to discuss understandings of God with our Buddhist friends

Chapter five deals with Buddhist and Christian understandings of self. We start with the Buddha's teaching on self and examine some teaching which emerged from a conversation between Saccaka and the Buddha. The Buddha encouraged Saccaka to take up meditation, as by doing so he would see inside himself and discover that what he thought was 'mine' was really 'not mine' and what he considered to be 'I' was really 'not I'. The Buddha went on to say that what the religious teacher Saccaka referred to as 'self' was not worthy of the designation 'self'. A very important function of non-self teaching (*anatta*) is not to establish a doctrine to be believed and defended—which would be just as bad as insisting on the concept of a 'self'—but rather to eliminate unhealthy self-interest and selfish behaviour. We also look at the well-known 'Chariot Story' where Nāgasena, the famous philosopher-monk, teaches King Milinda to take a more Buddhist understanding of 'self'. We will examine the Madhayamaka, Yogācāra and Zen understandings of self, as well as the Pudgalavadin position which challenged traditional Buddhist non-self teaching. Last, Christian understandings of self are explored through the writings of St Paul.

Chapter six begins by examining the Buddhist nature of *karma*. The idea of *karma* and the practice of the transfer of merit as an analogy of Jesus Christ suffering the penalty due to our shortcomings and transferring his righteousness to us is an approach which Christians have used with Buddhists for a considerable time. We go on to examine the substitutionary understanding of the atonement, with a focus on the sufferings of Christ. This leads to some questions: for example, did the Father abandon the Son on the cross of shame? Was it ethically acceptable for the Father to place the sins of the world on the Son?

The seventh chapter examines the implications of Christ's crucifixion and resurrection, and depicts him as the conqueror over the powers of darkness. The Apostle Peter talks about Christ bearing our sins in his body on the tree (I Peter 2:24). The word 'tree' (literally 'wood') is a euphemism for the cross, for there was a deep sense of shame and humiliation associated with crucifixion at that time. This 'Tree of Shame' may be seen as the heart of the Christian message. In a similar way, the 'Tree of Enlightenment' lies at the heart of Buddhism. It was under this tree that the Buddha allegedly realised the truth of all things and came up with a way for us to reduce our suffering. Indeed, from a Christian perspective, the cause and cessation of suffering is seen through the lens of the Tree of the Knowledge of Good and Evil (Genesis 2:9) and the Tree of Life. (Revelation 22:1-5) This latter tree constantly bears fruit and its leaves are for the healing of the nations. Of course, the tree is not the source of peace but a symbol of God's life-giving presence. It reminded us of the return of the cosmic conqueror to this world, when he will restore a suffering world to its original blissful state and bring about the cessation of all suffering. The end of suffering is a significant topic for Buddhists, given that the Buddha dedicated his life to discovering the cause of and solution to suffering and then teaching what he had discovered.

There is an appendix which describes the paths to enlightenment in the Theravāda and Mahāyāna traditions of Buddhism. This will serve as an introduction to those who are less familiar with Buddhist belief and practice.

About the author

It was a very hot Saturday morning back in 1983. A young western man got off his Suzuki motorbike in a park in the suburbs of Bangkok. There was a large group of Buddhist monks, nuns and lay people eating a vegetarian meal together. They were members of Santi Asoke, a group of Buddhists who were very critical of mainstream Thai Buddhism and were particularly strict in their own practice. The Santi Asoke members saw the young westerner and called out to him in English 'Come and eat with us—we will do you no harm.' The man, a missionary, did not want to join them, and roared off home on his motorbike.

Twenty years later, very close to that spot, a man in his early 50s knelt in front of a Santi Asoke monk and politely asked for permission to come and live with the community in order to learn its beliefs and practices. The monk didn't say anything; he just smiled, giving his consent.

The two events are connected because this is the same person. The change in attitude was brought about through the study of the life and work of Karl Reichelt. I know, because I was that person! In the intervening period I had left Thailand and as a postgraduate student at Edinburgh University, I came across the life of Reichelt. I began to look around and collect all the material that I could on his life and ministry. The material that I read inspired me to engage with the Buddhist world in a

About the author

completely different way. I moved from evangelism to enquiry, proclamation to conversation. And I often wondered how as a missionary to the Buddhist world for 12 years I had not come across Reichelt's story earlier.

But perhaps I should start at the beginning of my time living in Asia. I served as a church planting missionary in Thailand for 12 years with OMF International. In 1979, after initial language study, my wife, two small daughters and I moved out to a suburb of Bangkok to assist senior missionaries who were spearheading a church plant on a government housing estate. There were 100,000 people in that area, and there was no other church. Living conditions in the suburbs of Bangkok were fairly basic. This doubtless had something to do with being on a missionary stipend! We often had no running water in our small brick-built bungalow, which was a challenge for Rosalyn as she tried to keep our young daughters clean and cool. There was a public phone 300 metres away, but usually communication was by telegram. A highlight for my parents was a twice-yearly phone call from us and, of course, our weekly airmail.

We could not afford a car and often travelled locally on my Suzuki motorbike. Irresponsibly, I had two daughters perched on the petrol tank and Rosalyn sitting side-saddle behind me holding the youngest—who is now 34. I bought the bike from a military locksmith, an army sergeant who worked in a plain clothes surveillance team headed up by an army captain who was an emerging leader in the church. I am not sure if the vendor put aviation fuel into the petrol tank prior to me taking the Suzuki for a test run; it had remarkable, never to be repeated, acceleration. The most striking thing about the bike was the very short handlebars. When I asked the owner why they were so short, he told me that it was so he could squeeze himself between two lines of Bangkok traffic. I soon learnt to do that myself while carrying heavy loads of literature, films and groceries on the back of the bike!

After 12 years in Thailand we returned to the UK, but I soon missed Thailand. During my studies at New College at the University of Edinburgh, I came across the story and writings of Karl Reichelt (1877-1952), a Norwegian missionary to China. I identified some similarities between his background and mine. We were both brought up in strong Evangelical traditions and both felt a sense of call to be missionaries in Asia. I was fascinated by Reichelt's highly contextualised approach and his wide network of friends who were Buddhist monks. I read everything that I could lay my hands on about Reichelt and his ministry, and somehow, he gave me 'permission' to approach Buddhists in a different way. After completing my graduate studies I began to teach at a theological college and, amongst other things, introduced courses on Buddhism, Primal Religion and New Religious Movements. I saw the importance for personal academic development in the area of Buddhist studies and enrolled as a part time PhD student under the supervision of Professor Peter Harvey. In 2001, Thai missionary monks came to Edinburgh to open a Buddhist temple. We became friends and I enjoyed time with them, either at the monastery or in our home; helping in practical ways as best we could.

My doctoral studies took me back to Thailand for field work. My research topic was the study of two New Thai Buddhist Movements which emerged in the 1970s: the Wat Phra Dhammakāya and Santi Asoke fraternities. I was curious to find out what they believed and how they went about spiritual development. And why did they appeal to two very different types of the Thai middle class? The Santi Asoke Buddhist Movement, which by now had been excommunicated by the Thai *saṅgha*, had a major centre very close to the park where

I had, almost 20 years previously, turned down their monks' invitation to join them for lunch! As mentioned earlier, I went to the Santi Asoke centre in Bangkok and obtained permission to live in their communities and learn their ways. I remember on one occasion coming back from fieldwork at one of these centres feeling somewhat compromised in terms of my Christian faith and practice. It seemed as if I had spent most of my time listening to Buddhist sermons and kneeling in front of Buddhist monks. I shared my feelings with a Thai Christian friend, a colonel in the Thai army. He said 'Now you stand in the shoes of Thai Christians'. I found that to be a telling response. I had been a missionary for 12 years in Thailand, and had spent almost all of that time working with him—but now, for the first time, I was experiencing what it was like to be the only Christian living and working in an environment where almost everyone else was a Buddhist.

During my library research at a prestigious university for Buddhist monks, I approached one of the librarians asking for some advice regarding some Pali words. He was unable to help but looking up at an approaching Buddhist monk said 'You are in luck; here comes our Pali language specialist. Let's see what he says.' The Pali professor examined my document and said 'You really do need some help with this! Where are you staying?' When I told him that I was staying at a guest house he said, 'Save your money! Come and stay with me at my temple. I have a spare room.' I had never received such an invitation before! On the one hand, I was a conservative Christian, and a Buddhist temple was where I would go to borrow chairs if we had a big evangelistic event at the church! On the other hand, I remembered Reichelt's example of having many monastic friends and being warmly welcomed into many Buddhist temples.

Some days later, I nervously phoned up the scholar monk who had kindly invited me to stay with him at the very large Bangkok temple where he lived. He restated his invitation, and I moved from the guest house where I had been based into the spare room at the professor's *kuti*, or residence. I felt a bit like what I imagined Reichelt must have felt like as he stayed at temples, experiencing both hospitality and a very different way of living. I certainly experienced a real sense of belonging when temple security guards would sometimes stop me going in to the temple in the evening by saying, 'Excuse me, the temple is closed to tourists come back tomorrow.' I would reply, 'I know, but I live here. I am staying with the professor in *kuti* 18.' Some were a bit dubious and escorted me to where I claimed I was staying to make sure I really did live there! The scholar monk was very helpful; not only with language, but in providing me with a variety of contacts who were able to supply the information I needed for my research.

As I was completing my doctoral studies, the professor who had been so hospitable said to me, 'When you complete your research why don't you become a visiting lecturer at my university?' I remember asking 'Will that be OK? After all, I am a follower of Jesus and a student of Buddhism.' At that point he picked up my Bible and said 'That's all right. Together we can search for the truth'. I did spend two very rewarding summers living at the temple and lecturing on the MA International Programme on research methodology and Mahāyāna Buddhism.

Back in the UK, a combination of our contact with the Thai community, developing friendships with them, and offering Thai language Bible study have led to a number of Thai people recently being baptised. With many others, the friendships and conversations continue to grow. Terry Muck has put forward an interesting model of working with folks from other faith traditions: co-operation and competition. Traditionally, we Evangelical missionaries have found it easier to compete than to co-operate. After all, Christianity has a unique message—you can be right with God by trusting in Jesus to do for you what you cannot do for yourself. We cannot disregard Christ's command to go and help people to become life-long followers of Christ. In going, we address the needs of others; their *shalom* in this life as well as the life to come. Christianity is unique, and as Christians, we are called to co-operate in the mission of God and live in missionary encounter with the other.

But can we not also co-operate with those from different faiths? One reason to co-operate is that there are important issues in society which need to be addressed. And we do well to pool our resources and work together on issues of common concern, such as standing up against racism, opposing euthanasia, comforting the bereaved, being involved in environmental issues, helping AIDS sufferers and the homeless. By addressing these issues through working with people from different traditions, we get to know each other at a deeper level.

True, there are occasions when co-operation may lead us to compromise. These cut-off points are usually worked out by overstepping a boundary and we learn not to do that again. The very nature of being involved with people of other faiths at a deep level will lead us to be involved in situations where we are not in control, and sometimes we get carried into activities which we perceive to be a step too far. From these experiences, we continue to learn. This too is part of the journey.

Contents

Introduction ix
About the author xiv

1 **Lessons from the Life of Karl Reichelt** 1
Call to specialise in reaching out to Buddhists 3
Learning on location 4
Reichelt's ministry 5
Some aspects of Reichelt's ministry 10
Cost associated with Reichelt's ministry 12
Reichelt's missiology 14
Some limitations of Reichelt's missiology 19
Five lessons from Reichelt's ministry 22
Conclusion 31
Pause for reflection 32

I **God** 35

2 **The Buddha And Jesus Christ: Their Lives In 12 Acts** 37
Gotama's cultural and religious milieu 37
The 12 acts of the Buddha 41
Gotama's birth 42
Gotama's early life 44

	Gotama's quest for enlightenment	47
	The Buddha's enlightenment	50
	The teaching of the Buddha	52
	The *parinibbāna* of the Buddha	56
	The Life Of Christ In 12 Acts	59
	The early life of Christ	63
	Pause for reflection	75
3	**God And The Buddha**	**77**
	Did the Buddha point to aspects of God's work?	79
	Did the Buddha predict the coming of Jesus Christ?	83
	A Christian response to the Buddhist world	88
	Jeremiah, religious images and the nations	92
	Abraham's concern for the people of Sodom and Gomorrah	93
	Pause for reflection	98
4	**God and *Dhamma***	**99**
	Some Buddhist understandings of the *Dhamma*	100
	Venerable Buddhadasa's understanding of the *Dhamma*	104
	Jesus as *Dhamma*?	108
	What exactly do we mean when we say God is 'personal'?	112
	Should we compare God to the *Dhamma* or the Buddha?	118
	Conclusion	123
	Pause for reflection	124

II Self   125

5	**Buddhist And Christian Understandings Of Self**	**127**
	What did the Buddha mean by *anatta*?	128
	The Five Aggregates	129
	The *Culasaccaka Sutta*	133

The 'Chariot Story' 137
Madhayamaka understanding of self 139
The Yogācāra understanding of self 139
Some understandings of self in Zen Buddhism 141
A further reflection on 'mind-only' ideas 143
A summary of the main understandings of self within Buddhism 147
Humans as non-self but God as self: a conversation starter? 148
Toward an understanding of the Christian view of self 149
A perspective from St Paul 152
Pause for reflection 157

III Salvation   159

6 *Karma* And The Transfer Of Merit   161
Liberation in Buddhism: Salvation in Christianity . . 161
The writer's understanding of *karma* 166
Buddhist understandings of *karma* 168
The 'middle man' 174
A Buddhist response 179
Mahāyāna Buddhism and the transfer of merit . . . 183
Three paradoxes of the death of Christ 187
Conclusion 192
Pause for reflection 192

7 Christ's Triumph Over Dark Forces   195
The Tree of Shame and Christ's Triumph 196
The Tree of Life and the End of Suffering 203
Conclusion 206
Pause for reflection 207

8 Conclusion   209

God 210
Self 211
Salvation 212

Appendix 215
The Theravāda Tradition 215
The Emergence of Mahāyāna 217
Theravāda Stages of Spiritual Development 219
Three key differences 221
The Ten Stages of the Bodhisattva Path 223
The Path to Enlightenment in Zen Buddhism 227

Glossary of Buddhist Terms 233

Bibliography 241

Chapter 1

Lessons for Christian-Buddhist Conversation from the Life of Karl Reichelt (1877-1952)

Karl Reichelt spent his adult life as missionary in China. His critics say that his highly contextualised approach compromised the Christian message. His admirers suggest that his capacity to make and sustain cross cultural friendships coupled with his ability to create a non-threatening environment in which to explore the Christian faith were significantly used by the Lord. Whatever else, Reichelt was a risk taker. Now, some six and a half decades after his death, we examine Reichelt's life and work to see what we may learn about reaching out to the Buddhist world.

Karl Ludwig Reichelt was born in 1877 on a farm near Arendal, a city on the south coast of Norway. His father, a sea captain, died when Reichelt was very young. He was brought up by his mother who opened her home for house meetings and visiting preachers. Aged 18, Reichelt studied at a teachers' training college in Notodden where, according to Thelle (1981:66):

> [H]e encountered a more open, broadminded Christianity, which combined sound faith with a deep appreciation of humanity, nature, national traditions, and the culture of the people. Such attitudes certainly helped him later when he had to meet other cultures and learn to appreciate the other national and religious traditions of another people.

Two years later he entered the Missionary Training College of the Norwegian Missionary Society in Stavanger. He was ordained in Oslo in 1903, went on to complete a semester of medical studies in hospitals in the capital and arrived in China in November 1903.[1] After completing language study Reichelt worked in Hunan until 1911 when he returned to Norway after his eight year term of service.

---

[1] According to Strandenoes (2009:127), eight of the 1902 ordinands from the School of Missionary and Theology were ordained together in Oslo. On that occasion Reichelt preached from Acts 10:42-3.

Call to specialise in reaching out to Buddhists

In 1905, Reichelt made his first significant contact with the Chinese Buddhist world. He visited Weishan monastery which was situated in the mountains and was home to 400 Buddhist monks. Reichelt wrote home, 'As never before I have been able to look into a unique world, a world full of deep religious mystique, but also full of deep spiritual poverty.' (Sorik, 1997:73) Reichelt, along with his companions, spent one week in Weishan. They were treated with the friendliest hospitality he had ever experienced. This one week visit proved to be a life-changing event for the Norwegian missionary. Again he wrote:

> Sitting with the monks, desperately eager to tell them of the Gospel, he found that his words were not heard. They listened politely, but there was no echo. It was as if they lived in a different world; he could not speak to the framework of their thought. He realised that he was simply unprepared and from that time on he began to study Buddhism seriously. (Sorik, 1997:73)

Reichelt records another struggle he experienced on this visit. He was deeply burdened by the following question, 'Is it permissible for us to believe that God's Spirit can be at work within these bleak walls, where superstition and idolatry share space with the most exalted longings after truth, purity and freedom?' (Sorik, 1997:73) Towards the end of his week in the monastery, Reichelt believed that God spoke to him.

> It was as if I heard the Lord's voice. It came to me in the form which St Paul expressed it in the Acts

> of the Apostles, 'God is not far from any one of us for in Him we live and move and have our being', and 'God has not left himself without witness'. Long before missionaries came to China, God was in China. The glimpses of truth and points of contact you find he has placed there. (Sorik, 1997:74)

Reichelt concluded that what was necessary was serious study and went on to note 'I need not say that it was a changed missionary who walked down from the Weishan heights. It was a missionary whose heart was full of holy power and joy.' (Sorik, 1997:74)

Learning on location

Reichelt, having decided to devote his life to a special work among the Buddhists, began to study and observe Chinese Buddhism. He developed friendships with Buddhist monks and learned lay people alike. In fact, Reichelt wrote that the greatest obstacle in the relationship between the monks and the Christians was that Buddhist monks had found the followers of Christ (both missionary and national) lacking in a sympathetic and gentle attitude to others.

He returned to Norway in 1911. During this time he gave lectures on Chinese Religion. These lectures were published in 1913 and later translated as *Religion in Chinese Garment*. On his return to China in 1913, Reichelt was appointed New Testament Lecturer to the Chinese Union Lutheran Theological Seminary in Shekow. He taught there from 1913 to 1920 and used his vacations to visit temples and monasteries, making valuable contacts and collecting texts which he studied in order to gain deeper insight to Buddhism.

Reichelt's ministry

In 1919, at the large Pilu monastery in Nanking, a city he did not normally visit, Reichelt met several young monks who were interested in what he had to say. Kuantu, a 22 year old monk, who had a 'deep religious spirit' responded to the idea of the Great Saviour from Paradise. Eventually, Kuantu obtained leave from the monastery and spent several months with Reichelt reading the Bible, talking and praying. He was baptised on Christmas day 1919 and was soon followed by a small group of others, including his teacher Penchong, and the abbot of the temple. On 4th January, 1920, under Reichelt's leadership these new converts formed a 'Christian Brotherhood among China's Buddhists', based on the understanding that 'our Buddhist *Mahāyāna* scriptures point forward to Christianity as their true fulfilment.'

Clearly Kuantu's baptism and those who came to faith shortly afterwards must have seemed like the first fruits of things to come for Reichelt. True, others did follow, but not as many as was hoped for. Kuantu, the first convert, was young and gifted but did not fulfil Reichelt's expectations. Sharpe (1984:65) mentioned that Kuantu began to suffer from depression and wondered whether the culture shock of living in close proximity with westerners was not a trigger for his mental illness.

Reichelt returned to Norway for home assignment in 1920, full of optimism. He lectured in Scandinavian universities on Chinese Buddhism. His best known book, translated into English as *Truth and Tradition in Chinese Buddhism*, was based on his research and lecturing. In November 1922, Reichelt returned to China after his second home assignment in Norway. After some 17 years of preparation and with the support of the Norwegian Missionary Society Reichelt started a Christian community, a half-way house organised along the lines of a Buddhist monastery. It functioned as a 'Brother Home' or 'Christian Monastery' for religious seekers, especially Buddhist monks.

> The monks usually stayed for a couple of days, but could extend their stay if they wanted to continue the study of Christianity. Every year an average of 1000 monks visited the Brother Home in Nanking. Here they could encounter Christianity in an atmosphere adapted to their own traditions, and talk about religious problems with Christians who were familiar with their religion and, moreover, regarded them as spiritual brothers, and 'Friends in the Way'. (Thelle, 1981:67)

The following is a summary of some of the important aspects of the Brother Home (*Ching Fong Shan*). Wandering monks and pilgrims were received and, if it was felt that they were 'seeking', they were invited to stay for some weeks in the pilgrim halls. Indeed, if they were also young and well educated they would be invited to attend the school attached to the Brother Home. During the first year of the school programme there was a strong focus on religion. This study brought the students to a decision either to become Christian and generally to stay on, or to leave the school. Reichelt comments 'We on our side plead with them not to make a decision before they are perfectly clear about the consequences' (Reichelt, 1937:164). Following this there was a theological course which ran for three years. Reichelt (1937:164) went on to expand:

> In this way the baptized, gifted and promising men will get a training which in due time qualifies them for teaching, preaching, and pastoral work. In this course the ordinary theological curriculum is followed, special stress being laid upon the history of religion, the comparative study of religion and the psychology of religion.

In addition to this formal training many retreats were hosted at Tao Fong Shan, the Christian monastery founded in Hong Kong by Reichelt, and people from various religious backgrounds were invited by him and his colleagues to come and have informal but nevertheless serious discussions, and to 'sit down for earnest, religious talks and discussions'. (Reichelt, 1937:164)

Despite encouraging results from the outreach which took place at the Brother Home, the Norwegian Missionary Society had become uncomfortable with Reichelt's highly contextualised approach and what were said to be liberal ideas and syncretistic practice. 'Reichelt was left to choose between complete co-operation with the NMS or complete severance. Reluctantly Reichelt chose to work independently.' (Eilert, 1974:14) In January 1926, Reichelt formally parted company from the Norwegian Missionary Society and started the Nordic Christian Buddhist Mission, sometimes referred to as the Christian Mission to Buddhists.[2] From early on in the life of the Christian Mission to Buddhists, the symbol of a cross rising out of an open lotus flower was adopted. The lotus flower is one of the symbols of Buddhism and symbolises the Buddha as a person of integrity and a teacher of truth. It is really hard

---

[2] In 2000, the Nordic Christian Buddhist Mission became known as Areopagus.

to push a lotus leaf underneath the water; the part of the leaf you push down goes under the water while the rest of the leaf floats on the surface! And so integrity supports who we are and what we do. Of course, the cross represents Christianity. The symbol was intended to signify the planting of the gospel into the very heart of Buddhism. Eric Sharpe (1984:81) comments:

> To Reichelt—and this he had to explain time and time again in the next few years—the mission's symbol showed, first, that it was Christian, secondly, that it was directed towards Buddhists, and thirdly, that the 'new birth' comes only through the Cross.

Reichelt's critics saw the juxtaposition of these two religious symbols as syncretism, despite Reichelt's insistence that what was being signified was a missional approach. There were 31 registered 'wearers of the cross' between 1920 and 1931. Indeed, the cross continues to be worn round the neck by present day members of the mission.[3]

Between Christmas 1924 and Whitsunday 1925, two Buddhist monks had been baptised, along with a Taoist monk and 11 Buddhist novices (Sharpe, 1984:84). This, however, was a turbulent time as there was an escalation of anti-foreign feelings among the Chinese. In 1927, revolutionaries, in an anti-foreign rage, destroyed Ching Fong Shan; indeed Reichelt and his Norwegian assistant, Thelle, narrowly escaped with their lives. Riechelt decided not to open a new centre in China.

---

[3] On one of Reichelt's visits to Thailand, he was asked by a senior Thai official to remove the cross and the lotus symbol from around his neck before visiting a temple. It was felt that the symbol might well offend the monks given the way the cross was placed above the lotus flower. I am not sure how Reichelt responded.

After looking around a number of countries he thought it best to locate in Hong Kong. In 1930, a wooded hilltop was purchased from the government and Reichelt named it Tao Fong Shan, 'The Hill of the Christ Wind'. A Danish architect drew up plans based on Chinese monasteries and a beautiful complex was constructed that demonstrated a creative attempt to indigenise Christian worship.

Tao Fong Shan was a place where Reichelt researched Chinese Buddhism and developed his missionary thinking. He travelled extensively, once as far west as the borders of Tibet but also to other Asian countries. The first focus of Reichelt's ministry, however, was sharing the Christian message with religious visitors. He and his assistants invited monks from China for visits. Some became Christian, a number becoming workers in his mission. Reichelt (1937:163) comments:

> One of the most interesting gatherings in our institute on Tao Fong Shan is the weekly evening meetings, when sometimes pilgrims and students from the different regions of East Asia tell how they were guided to come to this mountain. Their thrilling tales prove that our journeys, the distribution of literature, the wide correspondence maintained and, last but not least, the accounts given by the monks who have been here are all means in the hands of God for upbuilding the coming Kingdom.

The Japanese invasion of China in 1937 put an end to monks visiting Tao Fong Shan. After Pearl Harbour, the Japanese captured Hong Kong and a period of hardship followed. Reichelt was allowed to continue at the monastery with his family and even carry on his ministry in the cathedral.

At the end of the war, Reichelt wanted to continue his work. He was, however, 69 years old, and not in the best of health. He returned to Norway, leaving his assistants to continue the ministry of the monastery. Political instability in China meant that a return to the old style of ministry became impossible as travel was considerably restricted. In 1939, Reichelt was awarded the St Olav medal by the Norwegian King Hakon VII for his meritorious work. Some two years later, he was honoured for his research on religious life in East Asia with an honorary doctorate from Uppsala University. (Strandenoes, 2009:129) In 1951, Reichelt returned to Tao Fong Shan on a short-term assignment. He did not return to Norway and in March 1952, Reichelt died of a brain tumour and was buried in the Resurrection Cemetery at Tao Fong Shan.

Some aspects of Reichelt's ministry

Toward the end of his address to the 1938 Third International Missionary Council in Tambaram near Chennai, Reichelt took the opportunity to talk about the experience he had gained over the previous 20 years of his contextualized ministry. During this time he had very close contact with thousands of ordained and lay Buddhists, Taoists and Confucians. Indeed, many of them had stayed at Reichelt's Christian monastery at Tao Fong Shan for months and, in some cases, years. He remarked that many of these men were contacted on his journeys, and those of his colleagues, to Buddhist centres and sacred mountains. Some of them, he said:

> become baptised Christians, a considerably greater number have not joined the Christian Church but continue to feed upon the words of the New Testament and are bound to Christ our Lord in deep

admiration, affection and love. These people have been acting as a vanguard for us in our work. (Reichelt, 1938:99)

Reichelt went on to explain how Jesus Christ became the centre of the lives of these people. They were all searchers for the truth and the religious experiences in their former religion more or less prepared them for coming to faith. These converts to Christ heard Christ's voice because they were on the side of truth (John 18:37). According to Reichelt (1938:99), 'in many cases it was just the Gospel of St. John which gave them the solution,' as it pointed to the new birth which brought entry into the Kingdom of God. This new birth was thrilling to many of the pilgrims. After years of meditation in lonely cells and strenuous pilgrimages to the holy mountains and visiting great religious teachers they broke through and entered into the experience they dreamt and longed for.

Reichelt (1938:100) concluded by saying:

> What I have experienced through these many years in the sacred hours of conversation with these people has given me the profound conviction that Christ has been working everywhere through all the ages. We should, therefore, gratefully and joyfully use the material which He Himself has prepared for the coming of His Kingdom. That the result is genuinely right is also clear. For Christ Himself has given us the criterion 'Ye shall know them by their fruits' (Matt.7:16): a circle of people who through faith in the Lord have been set free from sin, fear and bondage and are now enthusiastically giving up their lives in service for Him.

130 adults were baptized at Tao Fong Shan between 1930 and 1952. There were seven baptisms at Shanghai between 1940 and 1947 and there was one baptism at the Yuen Chau branch recorded in 1946 (Sharpe, 1984:204). Reichelt's ministry was not restricted to 'words', it also included deeds of compassion. Strandenoes (2009:136) refers to Reichelt's practice of giving food and money to those in need. He also tried to find employment for those who were out of work. His six months of medical and nursing studies in Oslo prior to his departure for China provided him with skills which he drew on in caring for the sick—those with serious wounds, and opium addicts who had attempted suicide.

Cost associated with Reichelt's ministry

In 1905, Reichelt married Anna Gerhardsen. The travelling involved in her husband's work and the political instability in East Asia meant she had to spend long periods in Norway away from her husband. 'It was not until after 1934 that she could be permanently with her husband and maintain a normal family life.' (Thelle, 1981:66) Riechelt returned by himself for what was meant to be a brief period in Hong Kong and died there in 1952. Separation must have involved considerable hardship for both of them.

Reichelt was severely criticised by many of his missionary colleagues. He was perceived by conservatives as being liberal. He drew fire not only from westerners but also from Chinese Christians who did not wish to be reminded of their previous religion. A common complaint aimed at Reichelt's approach was 'You go to the "Brother House" to learn about Christianity but all you get is Buddhism!' Reichelt's missiological approach, although currently admired by some practitioners, did not go down well at the Tambaram conference. Henrick Kraemer's (1888-1965) book published in time for the conference, *The Christian Message in a Non-Christian World*, criticised the fulfilment theology that was common in the 1920's and 30's, and described other faith systems as an effort to evade or placate God's wrath. Kraemer's views were generally accepted at the time and Reichelt's sympathetic approach to East Asian religion was viewed unfavourably by many missionaries. Kraemer mentioned Reichelt by name twice in his book. He praised the Norwegian missionary for interpreting Christianity to Buddhist monks but condemned any notion of Christianity being a more refined expression of Mahāyāna Buddhism. Reichelt felt criticized by this influential Dutch missiologist and frustrated that his careful defence of his mission to Buddhists was being challenged in a damaging manner. The two did meet on the train journey to the Tambaram conference, and subsequently corresponded. As Sharpe (1984:162) points out, Reichelt asked Kraemer for an indication that he believed Reichelt and his colleagues were 'trying to present the positive Christian Gospel in its full uniqueness to the Buddhist, not as a natural fruit of developed Buddhism, but as the unique and unspeakable gift from God'. Clearly, Reichelt felt that a testimony from Kraemer would avert any attack that Norwegian conservatives might launch on the mission as a result of Kraemer's negative published comments about Reichelt. Kraemer's response was friendly and he agreed that Reichelt was proclaiming the Gospel in its uniqueness rather than something that grew out of Pure Land Buddhism. He did not, however, go as far as Reichelt wished. The 'recommendation' was to make little difference, as by the time Reichelt received the letter the Germans had invaded Norway.

It was not only Christians who criticised Reichelt. His work drew fire from Buddhists who accused him of trying to damage the Buddhist community. He accepted, however, that 'the most violent opposition, the most biting outbursts of controversy and condemnation must be experienced by those who present the Christian message in Buddhist ranks' (quoted in Eilert, 1974:174). Thelle (2005:175) comments that 'a paradox inherent in such a dialogical mission is that the moment it really succeeds, it will lead to failure—the conversion of a great number of Buddhist monks would inevitably create barriers of mistrust and animosity.'

Reichelt's missiology

The central plank of Reichelt's approach to faith sharing is what he referred to as the 'Johannine approach'. This had as its focus the Prologue with its proclamation of the *Logos*. His position was that The Second Person of the Trinity is not to be restricted to the historical Jesus. There was never a time when the Son was not. Reichelt followed the approach of Justin Martyr, Clement of Alexandria, and Origen, in believing that the Eternal *Logos*, the Spirit of Christ, has revealed some truths to men and women of other faiths as they seek for truth. These divine truths, the *Logos Spermatikos*, are found in other religions and need to be identified and used to help those in these traditions come to an understanding of Christ.

Reichelt argued that the activities of the Son cannot be limited to the time since his incarnation. From eternity, he has functioned as the *Logos*. From the beginning He was abiding with the Father and was linked to the whole cosmos, and indeed, humanity after creation. He comments:

> All that is true, good and noble in all nations and races, in all cultures and religions, has accordingly

its origin in Him. What is the reason for this? The reason is that 'the light shineth in darkness' (verse 5). This is a permanent function on the part of the Logos through all ages, in all cultures and in all religions. (Reichelt, 1938:93)

According to Reichelt, as soon as the pre-existent Christ was recognised, Buddhists would acclaim their natural state as children of God. He 'had witnessed that such a discovery caused "an immense joy of recognition" among the converts'. (Eilert, 1974:135) There is a strong sense of optimism in Reichelt's missiology. He was looking forward to a new era when the Kingdom of God would come in a much fuller way. Tao Fong Shan was, for Reichelt, a resting place where the Kingdom of God could break through in the minds of those who visited. (Eilert, 1974:135) This optimism may well have been produced by post-millenarian beliefs; yet there are traces of the bodhisattva concept of Mahāyāna Buddhism informing Reichelt's practice.[4] But did he see himself and his colleagues as Christian bodhisattvas? He writes that 'the aim of mission, of world-salvation is therefore: to help all that belongs to Him to find its way back to Him again'. (Eilert, 1974:163) This is clearly in keeping with the bodhisattva's goal of striving for the liberation of all sentient beings. A bodhisattva is inspired and nurtured by the Buddhas; is there an echo of being nurtured by the Trinity to work for the liberation of all in the following comment of Reichelt?

> Fullness and vastness, and still no depressing feeling of loneliness. Because Merciful Divine Father embraces it all in the warmth of his love, a Saviour

---

[4] Post-millenarianists generally look forward to a 'golden age' of Gospel advance and peace on earth prior to the Lord's return.

and a Brother leads us along, and an all-pervading Holy Spirit fills our heart with peace and makes it possible for us to give ourselves up for the most sacred and blessed task which human thought can perceive the transformation of the whole universe into a Kingdom of God. (Quoted in Eilert, 1974:160)

Reichelt drew heavily on Buddhist concepts and terms. He looked at his own faith through the lens of Mahāyāna Buddhism, and used these reflections in his faith sharing. According to Sharpe (1984:71), Reichelt believed that Pure Land Buddhism's focus on receiving salvation as a free gift, as opposed to making merit through observing rituals, was partly due to the influence of the Nestorian Christian mission in China, and that he was simply building on the good work that God had done through that enterprise.[5] Reichelt refers to this influence as

'the sacred golden inheritance' which had left traces on Buddhist views of God, the notion of the Trinity, the belief in a Western Paradise, and much more besides. Thus in pointing to Jesus Christ

---

[5] Reliable evidence indicates that the first Christian missionaries to China were East Syrian or Nestorian Christians. This is based on the discovery of the Nestorian monument in China in 1625. The monument indicates it was erected in 781CE, mentions Nestorian doctrines, and gives a long list of missionaries (Sunquist, 2001:597). The Syriac-speaking Nestorian missionaries produced Christian literature, planted churches and established monasteries in China. The mission to China was pioneered by Alopen who arrived there in 635. The movement enjoyed the favour of the emperors and extended to the borders of Korea. Loss of sponsorship by the Emperor meant the church all but died out in the 10th century. It, however, experienced a resurgence from the 11th to 13th centuries, due to the support of the Mongol rulers who set up the Yuan dynasty, before falling into demise again.

as the 'fulfiller' of Mahāyāna Buddhism's best insights, Reichelt's language clearly owes much to the fulfilment school of Christian missionary thought, at that time chiefly operating in India. (Sharpe, 1984:71)

Thus Reichelt felt at liberty—indeed he considered it essential—to construct a liturgy where the Buddhist visitor would feel comfortable. Notto Thelle (2005:133) provides several clues to help us understand Reichelt's thinking. First, he writes that 'Reichelt regarded liturgical worship as the central expression of religious life.' Second, that Reichelt 'was influenced by the experience of "the holy" as described by Rudolf Otto (1869-1937) and Nathan Soderblom (1866-1931).'[6] Third, that 'the most characteristic and perhaps also the most important testimony to Reichelt's devotional piety was his extreme preoccupation with establishing sanctuaries for worship wherever he arrived.' Thelle recounts instances where Reichelt writes movingly that a sanctuary had been completed. These buildings received priority in the order of construction. Thelle (2005:136) also points out that Reichelt and his colleagues had the practice of taking their visitors 'first to the sanctuary to worship, to share some sacred moments, to pray or just be quiet, before they were introduced to the rest of the facilities. It might have been inspired by Buddhist practices. But it certainly revealed the overarching importance of the sanctuary in Reichelt's religious life.'

---

[6] Nathan Soderblom was a Lutheran minister and academic, a professor at Leipzig University. In 1914 he was elected archbishop and primate of Sweden. His interest in the Orient and his ecumenicalism, along with his pietistic upbringing, meant that he had a lot in common with Reichelt, who mentions him warmly in his writings and always remained appreciative of the Swede's support.

There are significant strengths in the traditional approaches to evangelism and establishing churches, in terms of the identity of new converts and what is acceptable in terms of behaviour. We do not want to jeopardise these strengths, nor do we want to confuse national believers. Yet, in some situations, it may be appropriate for those who feel called, to experiment with approaches which encourage dialogue between Buddhists and Christians. This may even include putting on residential programmes for them. A Christian Monastery approach, similar to that of Reichelt's "Brother Home", may be developed out of the new monastic community approach. In the West, we are currently witnessing the forming of new monastic communities, where people go and live in community in order to serve those within that geographical area; usually, the focus is on those on the margins of society. There is a commitment to extending hospitality and living according to a rule of life which usually involves contemplative practice. Such commitments to 'new style monastic living' do not have to be life-long, and families, couples and singles may be part of these new monastic communities. Would it be possible to develop a ministry to Buddhists, either in the west or in Asia using this model of new monastic communities? A rule of life could be devised which prioritises times of individual and corporate contemplation, the offering of hospitality to the outsider, mindfulness in practical work and the chanting of the Christian Scriptures. Frankly, this would appeal to many spiritual seekers who are looking for a community in which to explore spirituality.

Another way of reaching out to monastic communities would be to open study centres near universities for Buddhist monks and nuns. For some years, the Seventh Day Adventist Mission in Thailand operated such a centre just opposite a prestigious Buddhist university in Bangkok. Local and international students alike went to the centre to use the computers, browse through the small library and discuss their academic work with staff. The centre also had a fine display of Thai art depicting biblical scenes. This innovative project generated goodwill not only among its service users but also its neighbours, and it was very sad to hear of its closure due to lack of finances.

The 'new monastic' approach and the study centre may not be feasible in all contexts, due to a lack of finance or personnel. A more organic and modest approach might be both possible and successful in terms of developing friendships with Buddhists. Visiting a teaching temple or institution of higher learning and getting to know some of those who are responsible for teaching would be a start. It is most likely that they would welcome someone who could come in to teach English, or offer an occasional class on the Christian faith or some aspects of it. This could be the start of some significant friendships as well as providing fascinating insights into monastic culture. In the West, Buddhist temples function as community centres for the Asian diaspora. There are opportunities to help in a variety of ways and be involved in what is going on in the local community. My own initial involvement was in the area of translating documents and helping with transport. I was invited to be involved in the care of the dying and helping to arrange funerals. As a result of these activities, I made many good friends and learnt much about Buddhist belief and practice.

Some limitations of Reichelt's missiology

Reichelt certainly studied hard to understand the world view of his audience and his approach was one of genuine friendship and inquiry. There were, however, some limitations. In my opinion he had an excessively high view of Pure Land Buddhism. Like the Welsh Baptist missionary Timothy Richard (1845-1919), he understood Pure Land to be the purist form of Buddhism.[7] On the one hand, Reichelt esteemed Richard as a person who wrote positively about Pure Land Buddhism and identified points of contact between this tradition and Christianity. On the other hand, Reichelt called Timothy Richard 'spirit-filled, but often far too bold'. (quoted by Sharpe, 1984:71) Both missionaries viewed Mahāyāna Buddhism as superior to the Theravāda tradition, and Pure Land Buddhism was seen as the highest expression of Mahāyāna Buddhism because of its emphasis on the concept of faith in someone other than one's self for salvation. Reichelt believed that Mahāyāna pointed beyond itself and ultimately found its fulfilment in Christ. (quoted in Eilert, 1974:164) This type of fulfilment approach—and indeed, the using or reloading of Buddhist terms with Christian meaning—requires careful thought. Any building on or 'borrowing' may be viewed by Buddhists as Christianity colonizing Buddhism.

The concept of grace shines very clearly out of Pure Land Buddhism, particularly as every other expression of Buddhism focuses on liberation through self effort. Indeed, when the Jesuits arrived in Japan around 1580, they were shocked by the similarity of Pure Land Buddhism to Protestantism. In dismay they exclaimed 'Martin Luther has been here before us!'[8]

---

[7] Pure Land Buddhists believe that trusting in the Amitabha (Amida) Buddha means one will be reborn in his Pure Land, Sukhāvatī, in the western region of the universe. This rebirth is not due to personal *karma* but rather a transfer of Amitabha's merit to the believer brought about by prayer and trust. Enlightenment may be gained more easily in this final life in Sukhāvatī because of the conducive conditions which exist there, in particular being taught by Amitāba himself.

[8] For an interesting account of the Jesuit mission in China and Japan see Andrew Ross (1994). *A Vision Betrayed: The Jesuits in Japan and China 1542 – 1742.*

While Reichelt engaged with a number of key Buddhist concepts on their own terms and used them as a lens to examine his own Christian faith, the association of All Father or Christ with Amitābha, the Buddha of the Pure Land, is very much a penultimate arrangement and best to be avoided. For example, there was a time when the Amitābha Buddha was Dharmakara, a bodhisattva seeking enlightenment; at this point, a comparison with Christ breaks down.

While not a missiological issue, we note that Reichelt did not respond well to criticism. In an interesting article about his father Notto Normann Thelle (1901-1990), Reichelt's right hand man, Notto R Thelle (2008:84) writes that Reichelt did not welcome discussions about strategies and theological positions with his staff. He 'never checked the opinions of new staff, but he nevertheless expected them to share his views.' Indeed, Johannes Prip-Moller, the Danish architect who designed Tao Fong Shan, felt that 'Reichelt's tendency to micromanage was an oppressive deprivation of freedom' and that his vision and empathy with others were 'limited exclusively to the sphere of religion'. Indeed, he said that Reichelt regarded disagreement as 'personal invalidation'. It is—thankfully—unlikely that Reichelt would get away with this kind of behaviour nowadays with new missionaries. If Prip-Moller's comments are true, then one can imagine the impact that criticism from colleagues, the Norwegian Missionary Society, and the wider missionary community must have had upon Reichelt.

Edinburgh: Edinburgh University Press.

Five lessons from Reichelt's ministry

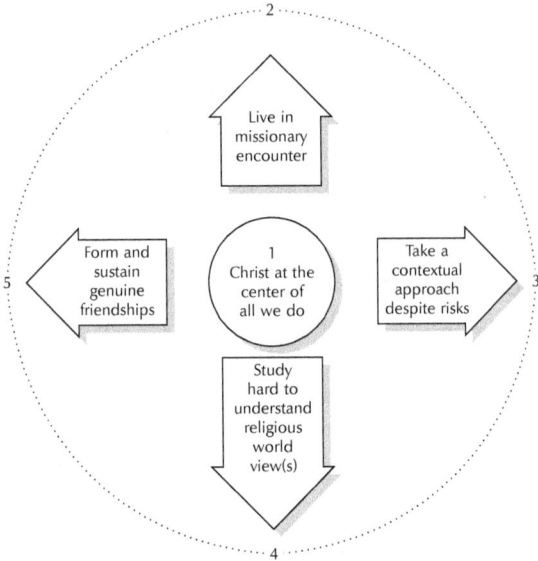

First, Riechelt appears to have prioritised the keeping of Christ at the centre of his life and ministry. He ends an article written in 1937 entitled *Buddhism in China Today* with the following words:

> We have one great aim, namely, to give the full Christian message, the full positive Gospel as it is revealed in the New Testament, using all the points of contact which psychologically may help the seekers after truth in East Asia to recognise Jesus Christ as the only way to the Father. We can afford to be broadminded because our work is through and through Christocentric.

At an Areopagus summer gathering in Denmark in July 2013, several scholars familiar with the work of Reichelt indicated that he had read widely and, in some cases, with approval in the areas of Theosophy and Anthroposophy. This has documented, for example, by Filip Riisager.[9] Unfortunately, however, this and other relevant materials have not been published in English and until they are, I am dependent on the verbal comments of Scandinavian specialists. From these conversations it would appear that Reichelt genuinely saw a cosmic dimension to Christ's rule, and tried to shape his christological understanding so that those within the Theosophical and Anthroposophical movements would be open to a theologically conservative understanding that Jesus of Nazareth is God come in human form, and that there was only ever one incarnation of Jesus who is also the Christ. This is in opposition to some esoteric teachings within those traditions, in which Jesus is viewed as one of many messengers or projections of the Cosmic Christ or the 'Solar Logos' into this world. For example, Benjamin Crème, a present day channeller of Maitrea and founder of Share International makes a clear distinction between Jesus and Christ. Crème views Jesus as just one of the many incarnations of the Christ, who is, like everything else, still evolving spiritually—nothing is perfect, everything is evolving, even the Christ. So, according to Crème, "the Christ" is more spiritually advanced now than when he walked the earth as Jesus.

Reichelt found aspects of the cosmic dimension of Christ both attractive and biblical, and allowed his Christological perspective to be influenced by some non-Christian views. That said, he explicitly denied that the historical Jesus was separate

---

[9] His *The Lotusblossom and the Cross* (1998) goes into considerable detail regarding Reichelt's engagement with writings from the Theosophical Society.

from Christ, and offered a sophisticated description of Christ which demonstrated knowledge of esoteric Christological understandings of the mid 1900s. Evangelicals rightly offer a staunch defence of the uniqueness of Jesus, but sometimes this is restricted to teaching within the church, rather than in a context of mission to non-Christians. These affirmations of faith also need to be given—in a nuanced manner and in the context of friendship—to those who identify themselves as having a New Age background. For the Evangelical, part of reflecting on missionary practice involves ensuring that we are both being faithful to the biblical text and the missionary task. That is, between a contending 'for the faith that was once for all entrusted to the saints' (Jude 3) and being 'all things to all men so that by all possible means I might save some'. (1 Corinthians 9:22; see Tyra 2013:12)

We will be helped in our task of achieving and maintaining a missional orthodoxy—living between the two book-ends of Jude 3 and I Corinthians 9:22—by involvement in an ongoing theological conversation with someone who understands our quest for good contextualisation but is also theologically aware. This theological conversation, together with dependence on the Spirit, reflection on Scripture, and a critical reading of the writings of those from our audience, can only enhance our capacity to communicate Christ in ways that are relevant. We will often find that this kind of reflective practice also re-enchants our walk with God, and this in turn contributes to our witness to Him.

Second, Reichelt was genuinely interested in Buddhism but lived in missionary encounter with Buddhists. Reichelt's friendship with Buddhist communities was a new approach in the 1920s and 30s. He did not take a condemnatory approach toward Buddhists, but rather engaged with them and learned as much as he could about Buddhism. Despite his high view of some elements of Buddhist teaching and his personal affection for Buddhists, he was able to maintain a posture of missionary encounter with Buddhists. At the same time, he did not always approve of the monastic communities he and his companions visited. For example, he wrote in disparaging terms about ten Tibetan-style Buddhist monasteries that he visited in Mongolia in 1937, and referred to black magic activities behind the scenes (Sharpe, 1984:149). In the same year, he visited Siam (Thailand) and found the Theravāda tradition there 'narrow and unimpressive.' (Sharpe, 1984:149) Clearly, the further Reichelt moved away from Pure Land Buddhism, the less positive he was about Buddhist belief and practice.

In a talk at Tambaram, Reichelt indicates that despite his contextualized approach he had not parted company from the Evangelical position:

> I also hold the view that in our witness we must never lose sight of the great truths in regard to personal salvation so strongly set forth by St Paul, such as sin and grace, redemption through Christ, the living faith which sets us free and makes us partakers of the Heavenly Kingdom, with its wonderful vision of life in time and eternity. (Reichelt, 1938:91)

More recently, Norwegian scholar Notto Thelle describes Reichelt as a 'pilgrim missionary':

> As a missionary he was convinced that he had a special calling to preach, with a particular vision of a mission to Buddhists. Whatever he did as a student of religion, a dialogue partner, and a

preacher—he wanted to share his faith with others. He seemed to use every opportunity to deliver his message, expecting some of the monks to be prepared to grasp the gospel. (Thelle, 2005:115)

Third, Reichelt took a contextual approach despite the risks of being misunderstood by fellow believers. Riechelt's monastery was a place where Buddhist monks were made welcome, he and his assistants wore Buddhist-type robes, and the food was vegetarian. He developed forms of worship that would not be unfamiliar to the Buddhist monks. There was the burning of incense, bells were rung and selected Buddhist scriptures were studied and related to the Bible, which was understood to be the supreme standard.

The Norwegian missionary wrote hymns and prayers that were couched in Buddhist terms. Indeed, he would often translate 'God' for the Buddha. One example of Reichelt's boldness is found in a hymn to Christ included in a book of liturgy used at the Brother Home. In this hymn, Christ is worshipped as 'The Great *Tao* without beginning and end, the eternal Word of God), and the original face of all sentient beings'—a Zen idea but alluding, at least in Reichelt's mind, to the concept of the *imago Dei*. Japanese Buddhist scholar and Zen practitioner DT Suzuki (1870-1966), commenting on Reichelt's centre and the ethos of the worship there, described it as a 'refined, religious atmosphere indigenous to the religious soul of China'.[10]

Buddhist practice usually begins with the reciting of the Triple Gem:

---

[10] Reichelt had a high view of Suzuki as a scholar and a Buddhist practitioner. Eilert (1974:126) comments that in 1927 Reichelt 'was happy to meet Suzuki whose books I have read so often'. Indeed, Eilert goes on to suggest that there is an element of Zen to be seen in Reichelt's writing, which suggests that he was influenced by Suzuki.

> I take refuge in the Buddha.
> I take refuge in the *Dhamma.*
> I take refuge in the *Saṅgha.*

Reichelt believed that a Christian equivalent to the Triple Gem was necessary to help visiting monks understand that worship was taking place and proposed the following (a prototype of which he found in a Nestorian liturgy).

> I take refuge in the Father of all goodness and mercy.
> I take refuge in the mysterious, perfect Law. (*Tao/Logos*)
> I take refuge in the shining pure Holy Spirit. (Sorik, 1997:76; Sharpe, 1984:81)

Reichelt had a strong emphasis on the confession of sin and there were confessions each evening and in the Sunday morning service.[11] Indeed, for Reichelt, 'Saturday afternoons were often set aside for the preparation for the Sunday morning worship, with strong emphasis on serious reflection on one's sins, contrition, and commitment to a new life' (Thelle, 2005:153). Indeed, Thelle goes on to cite a hymn used at Tao Fong Shan prior to the confession of sin:

---

[11] Yet Eric Sharpe (1984:200) relates a comment from Notto Normann Thelle, who thought that Reichelt did not fully enter into the activities of the Oxford Group Movement because he found it difficult to confess sin in front of others. Reichelt and his colleagues engaged with the Oxford Movement in Scandinavia, but also in Hong Kong. (The Oxford Group was later called The Moral Re-Armament Group.) The Oxford Group developed absolute standards of purity, unselfishness, honesty and love amongst its members through house parties which included discussions, testimonies and confession of sin.

> Christ, give me a shining lamp.
>
> And remove the karmic hindrances, that [I may] obtain eternal life/birth.
>
> The sentient beings are innumerable, [my] vow is inexhaustable:
>
> I will dedicate myself to return the Lord's favour to innumerable lands.

Here the confessor prays that the shining lamp of the Christian Scriptures will remove all fetters which hold the believer back from spiritual development. Karmic hindrances is a term used for sin or unskilful action. The last two lines resonate with the bodhisattva vow. Thelle (2005:154) comments:

> Reichelt was impressed by the Buddhist vow to save all sentient beings, and adopted the expression as part of his own missionary urge: the flavour of forgiveness should be proclaimed to the whole world, or literally, to the innumerable lands.

As already mentioned, Reichelt came under attack for his efforts at contextualisation. He was well aware of the dangers of an over-contextualised approach, yet was prepared to take risks in 'borrowing' from the other tradition, as was clear from his comments:

> Syncretism and compromises in mission work are a real danger which missionaries must continuously guard against. On the other hand it is equally certain that there is a great danger lest they neglect to make use of the sacred material

which Christ through His Spirit has made available in the life of the peoples and in their historical heritage. (Reichelt, 1953:59)

He sometimes became more cautious as a result of the comments of his critics. That said, Reichelt was not overly concerned about the lines of demarcation between Christianity and other faiths. His first focus was making Christ known to Buddhists in terms they could best understand. If we were to use sociological 'set theory,' we may say that Reichelt operated a 'centred set' rather than a 'bounded set' approach. That is, attendees belonged to the group before they accepted the group's core values.[12]

Those who stayed at the Brother House were encouraged to ask questions about core values, and to observe both individuals and the way the Brother House functioned as a whole. In this sense, they belonged to the community although they did not yet believe. Some contemporary understandings of conversion/discipleship believe that discipleship could well

---

[12] For an good introduction to 'sets', see pp.180-2 of Stuart Murray (1998). *Church Planting*. Milton Keynes: Paternoster Press. The Brother House operated on a 'centred set' approach, described in the text, while some churches operate on a 'bounded set' model. A bounded set approach operates with clear boundaries and maintains the integrity of the community by excluding any whose beliefs or behaviour are unacceptable. New members are inducted into the doctrinal beliefs and practices of the church. An advantage of this approach is that it provides structure and order, and that issues are black and white. A disadvantage may be that the setting of excessively rigid boundaries may marginalise people who have questions about belief and/or practice. Emphasizing a culture of conformity for whatever reason may unnecessarily marginalize people, or they may marginalize themselves by coming to believe that they cannot belong to the group.

A third approach would be the 'fuzzy-set'. Not only is this model without significant boundaries, it has no clear values at its centre. A wide range of behaviour is tolerated in this approach and there are dangers of compromise and confusion associated with this.

precede conversion and that for many the journey to faith resembles the Emmaus Road rather than the Damascus Road.

I have just returned from a Bible study with a Thai friend who is just completing a PhD. He is very impressed with the teachings of Jesus and experiences what he describes as 'God's power' as he spends time with Christians who are working together. Culturally he is Buddhist, but is exploring what it would mean for him to be a Christian. He feels the need for a 'space' between his Buddhist-informed culture and the Christian church. He would like to feel part of a group of people, Christians and not-yet Christians, with whom he can discuss his questions and begin to apply new ideas to his life. Church attendance is often "too much, too soon" for many not-yet Christians and, in certain situations, we would do well to ask the seekers we know what this penultimate, middle space might look like.

Fourth, Reichelt took the religious tradition of his audience very seriously and studied hard to understand it. Despite study and intellectual enquiry Reichelt always appeared to be missional. Moreover, we can see how Reichelt's interest opened up unusual opportunities for both himself and his colleagues. It may be that you sense an interest in reaching out to Buddhist monastic communities. Or, perhaps you wish to improve your understanding of the religious world view of those you have been called to minister to. I imagine that as you move forward in either of these areas you will develop deep friendships through your questions, listening and conversations. This leads us on to the next lesson we learn from Reichelt.

Fifth, Reichelt formed and maintained genuine friendships; indeed he had what can only be described as a special gift for friendship with religious people from East Asia. He was often invited to speak at religious associations in temples and monasteries. In many cases some of the monks in a temple had already visited the "Brother Home"; in others, rumours about the Christian "Master" had reached the temple in advance. Indeed, Gluer (1968:56) goes as far as to say that 'the secret of Reichelt's success in his encounter with Buddhists was not in his theological principles but in his warm personality.'

Yet we cannot divorce Reichelt's theology from his personality. His openness to those of different faiths and his vision to offer generous hospitality on a 'no-strings attached' basis facilitated the creative experiment that we refer to as the Brother Home.

Conclusion

Missionaries from more theologically conservative traditions may experience a 'calling' to reach out to those from another religious tradition and may wish to seriously study that religion. They may, however, feel that such serious study is not in keeping with a conservative position. To such, Reichelt offers 'permission'! With Christ at the centre of life and ministry, one can be comfortable with a measure of openness at the circumference. We can, in time and with God's help, discover what is appropriate contextualisation. Clearly, our approach will vary from situation to situation, and the extent to which we feel able to contextualise may well vary as our understanding of the missional task changes.

Those who come from a background influenced by postmodern values, or from a less theologically conservative position, may need to be encouraged to be more evangelistic as they engage with others. In terms of engaging with people of other faiths, Terry Muck (2000:43–44) suggests an approach of both 'cooperation and competition'. We cooperate because we have issues of common concern and can help each other achieve a particular outcome; some examples may include clean water supplies, a better education system and improved health care. We compete—and maybe that is too combative a word—because we have distinct belief systems and consider these to be crucial for the 'here and now' as well as 'after death'. Indeed, in our relationships, we also allow those who hold different beliefs to 'compete' *with us*. Our friendships are not predicated on having the same religious beliefs but on relationships that have been built up over time.

In Reichelt's life and ministry, we are reminded that if we maintain our relationship with Christ, his love will be in our hearts. If Christ's love is in our hearts, then the people we are called to will be in our hearts. If they are in our hearts, then we will be in their hearts.

Pause for reflection

1. What activities help you to keep Christ at the centre of who you are and what you do? For example: silence, Bible intake, attending church services.

2. If you take a highly contextual approach in reaching out to others, what checks and balances have you been able to build in to ensure that you do not over contextualise?

3. Footnote 12 on page 29 mentions set theory. Are there changes you could make in your ministry to open up 'space' to the people who you are trying to reach?

    Or, think of the Buddhist monks and nuns in your area. How might you begin to get to know them? It may be that there is a teaching monastery, or a Buddhist university nearby. Can you visit and see if there are ways of being of service?

Part I

God

Chapter 2

The Buddha And Jesus Christ: Their Lives In 12 Acts

This chapter will look briefly at the context in which the Buddha grew up and taught. The life of any Buddha is often discussed under 12 separate headings. I have wondered if it would be helpful to Buddhists if Christians were to describe the life and ministry of Jesus Christ through the use of 12 comparable acts or stages.

The cultural and religious milieu into which Gotama was born

Around 1500 BCE, the Aryans, a nomadic people, came from what is now northern Iran and southern Russia into north-west India. They spoke dialects of old Indo-Aryan (Sanskrit).

Once in India their influence gradually spread southwards and eastwards from the Punjab. By the time the one who would be known as the Buddha was born, the Aryans had been in India for around 1,000 years. Their coming did not bring political unity but an ideology which shaped Indian thought. The religion of the Aryans was based on its Scriptures known as the *Veda*, 'knowledge'—in this case, sacred knowledge.

An important concept in Aryan thinking—and indeed contemporary Hinduism—is that of *Brahman*. Knott (1998:17) points out that originally this referred to 'creative power or truth, inherent in the *Vedic* hymns and later in the sacrifice, during which they were recited. By the time of the early *Upanishads* it had come to refer to the cosmic principal or absolute reality.' Harvey (1990:10) adds:

> *Brahman* is seen as the substance underlying the whole cosmos, and as identical with the *atman*, the universal self which the yogic element of the Indian tradition had sought deep within the mind. By true knowledge of this identity, it was held that a person could attain liberation from reincarnation after death, and merge back into *Brahman*.

The central practices of what we now refer to as Hinduism are priests (Brahmins) conducting religious ceremonies, the singing of praises to *devas* (gods), and the placing of sacrifices into a sacred fire. The Brahmins officiate at these ceremonies and are assisted by non-Brahmins. Through these rites it was hoped to gain success in this life and life after death with the help of the god to whom the sacrifice was made. Brahminical practice included the repetition of sacred texts known as *mantras*. This practice helped to secure success and safety by requesting a particular god to provide what was required.

The function of the Brahmins then was to preserve the truth (*sruti*) that had been heard by the wise men. Gombrich (1988:33) comments that '*Sruti* is eternally true and infallible. It tells men what to do. Since it is the prerogative of Brahmins to learn and interpret it, all authority on ultimate matters rest with them.'

We have mentioned the Brahmins, but other members of Vedic society in descending order of status (and purity) are the *Kshatriyas*, the warriors-rulers whose duty is to maintain order and, where necessary, inflict appropriate punishment. Third, there are the *Vaishyas* whose duty is to generate wealth through farming and trade. Fourth, there are the *Shudras*, or servants, and below this are a group known as the Outcasts who prefer to be referred to as Dalits. They are considered to be particularly unclean because of their habits and occult practices. Of course, not all Brahmins were full-time priests, but they did officiate at rituals and enjoyed significant privilege in society as guardians of truth.

Three major assumptions emerged from the *Upanishads*, the secret Scriptures passed on from the more orthodox wandering teachers (*samaṇas*) to their pupils. They are as follows, first: monism, the assumption that all that exists is one, and that an element known as *Brahman* supports the whole cosmos. Second, that the human soul is part of *Brahman* and so must be eternal. Third, reincarnation, the idea that a life passes from one form of existence to another and assumes different forms depending on the *karma* associated with it. *Karma* continues to be an essential feature of brahmanic thought. Romila Thapar (1986:46) writes that the doctrine of *karma* 'is the philosophical justification for caste—souls are born to happiness or success according to their conduct in their previous life'.

Around the time that the Old Testament was being brought to a conclusion, approximately 480BCE, the man who was to become the Historical Buddha was born. The region where he was born was going through a period of change, in a number of ways. First, small communities were being drawn into larger ones which in turn became city states. Second, the concentration of many people living together caused increased disease. Third, expensive sacrifices and the oppressive control of the caste system made Brahmanism unpopular amongst non-Brahmins.

Another important distinctive of the time was that there were many wandering philosophers who lived ascetic lives and relied on the giving of those who listened to their teaching. These wandering teachers sought to bring meaning to life; they had given up their family and economic responsibilities and travelled around practising forms of yoga, meditation and self mortification.

We now look briefly at four ideological groups which functioned around the time of the Buddha. First, there were the Jains, who were founded around the time of the Buddha and led by Vardhamana the Mahāvira, or Great Hero. This fraternity believed that all things contain a life-principal or soul (*jiva*). The aim of this tradition is to set free the life-principal from rebirths by using ascetic practice such as fasting to get rid of previous *karma*, and to avoid generating negative karmic actions by exercising non-harmful action to all sentient life. Harvey (1990:13) comments that 'while the Buddha agreed with the Jains on such matters as rebirth and non-violence, he saw their theory of *karma* as somewhat mechanical and inflexible, and opposed their asceticism as too extreme'.

A second group were the Ajīvakas, who were founded by Makkhali Gosāla, a contemporary of the Buddha. Gosāla took the view that humans had no ability to affect their future lives by their good actions. Indeed, all actions were influenced by an impersonal destiny, *niyati*. This is significantly different from the Buddhist concept of *karma*, which states that our future is shaped by human action and its related outcome. Skilful action for the Ajīvakas involved accepting their destiny and carrying out ascetic practices.

The third group we mention are the Materialists who denied rebirth and *karma*. Those within this fraternity took the view that at death the person or creature was annihilated. The Materialists aimed to live a balanced life where relationships and simple pleasures were enjoyed.

Last, there were the Skeptics. They maintained that questions about life after death could not be adequately answered—this knowledge, at least for them, was impossible. The Buddha viewed the Skeptics as 'eel-wrigglers' due to their lack of commitment to any position. I am sure, however, that he would have appreciated their view of the importance of firm evidence before making a commitment to a particular belief! Harvey (1990:14) reminds us that the Buddha's two chief disciples, Sariputta and Moggallana, were originally members of the Skeptic fraternity.

The 12 acts of the Buddha

Often in Mahayana Buddhism, the life of a Buddha is arranged in 12 significant stages or acts. They are as follows:

1. The resolve to be born.
2. The bodhisattva descends from the Tuṣita heaven.
3. The bodhisattva enters Maya's womb.
4. The birth.
5. The accomplishments of the Buddha as he grew up.
6. The life of pleasure.

7. The great renunciation.
8. Ascetic practices.
9. The conquest of Māra.
10. The enlightenment that is the attainment of *nirvāṇa* and buddhahood.
11. The teaching of the Buddha.
12. The Buddha's passing into *pariṇirvāna*.

Gotama's birth

It is said that the man who came to be known as the Buddha had already experienced thousands of reincarnations over millions of years. He knew life as an animal, a person and as a god. It is also said that a hundred thousand eons ago, the Buddha to be, who at that point in time was an ascetic named Sumedha, was inspired to be a bodhisattva through a meeting with Dipankara, a previous Buddha.

The *Jātaka* is a collection of 550 stories about the Buddha in his previous lives. One of the stories concerns Gotama, the Buddha of this age, waiting in heaven for many eons for the auspicious time for his arrival on earth. This resolve to be born is *the first act of a Buddha*. At the appropriate time the Buddha-to-be selected as his mother Mahāmāyā, who showed her purity in many previous lives. She had made a vow of chastity and one night dreamed that a small white elephant entered her womb through her side. This descent from the Tusita heaven and the entering into his mother's womb represents *the second and third act of a Buddha*.

Ten months later in a grove of trees at Lumpini, on the Nepalese side of the current boundary between Indian and Nepal, Mahāmāyā gave birth to the Buddha-to-be. The earth allegedly trembled and supernatural beings were present at the birth. The birth, then, is *the fourth act of a Buddha*. Unlike in China, dating was not deemed to be important in India during that period. The Buddhist tradition says that the Buddha died when he was 80 years old. Older sources suggest a date in the 480s BCE for the passing away (*parinibbāna*) of the Buddha. This is based on a particular Sri Lankan account of teachers since the time of the Buddha. Newer sources, however, place the passing of the Buddha near to 400BCE and so a birth date of 480BCE may be assumed.

The Buddha's father was named Suddhodana. He appears to have been a nobleman whose turn it was to rule over his tribe for 12 years. The tribe was the Shākya clan, a community who lived in the region of Kosala. The city of Kapilaavatsu, in the Himalayas was the stronghold of this tribe. The powerful Magadha kingdom to the north was a threat to the Shākya and other tribes at the time. The Buddha-to-be was named Siddhattha Gotama.[1] He was allegedly born out of Mahāmāyā's side, and immediately took seven steps towards the four cardinal points of the compass, declaring that this would be the last time he would be born. Immediately after Gotama's birth, a lotus flower sprung up at each of these points. Mahāmāyā died seven days later; it is said that she who gives birth to a Buddha may never serve any other purpose. Gotama was brought up by his mother's sister, Mahāpajāpati who became Gotama's father's wife.

There are various accounts of wise men who attended the rituals and celebrations of the birth of Gotama. One notable

---

[1] Pali spelling. Sidhattha means 'one who has achieved his aim' while Gotama (Pali; Sanskrit 'Gautama') is a clan name. The Buddha is also referred to in Mahāyāna Buddhism as Shākyamuni, 'the sage of the Shākya clan', referring to the tribe into which the Buddha-to-be was born. 'Buddha' is a title for one who is completely aware of all that is happening, one who is fully awake or enlightened.

account tells of the astrologer Asita, who attended the naming ceremony of Gotama five days after the child's birth. The astrologer, perhaps drawing on psychic powers, noticed the physical marks on Gotama of a future enlightened being or great ruler—the circular pattern on his feet and fingers, and toes joined by webs. Asita indicated that if Gotama saw 'four signs of what life was like,' then he would forsake the royal life and become an enlightened being. If he did not see these signs, then Gotama would become a world monarch. The signs, referred to as 'the Four Passing Sights', were old age, sickness, death and a wandering ascetic. Gotama's father had ambitions for his son to become a mighty ruler, and so protected him from these sights by keeping him within the palace compound and only allowing him out on carefully choreographed trips.

Gotama's early life

There is a story of Gotama as a young lad, attending a ploughing ceremony where his father was officiating. Gotama had been absorbed in meditation for some hours and it seemed to those present that during this time the sun stood still. Another story recounts how Gotama's cousin, Devadatta, shot a swan in flight and how Gotama ran forward to pick it up and nurse it back to health. The accomplishments of a young Buddha-to-be are seen as *the fifth act of a Buddha.*

Aged 16, Gotama married Yasodharā. His father built three palaces for the newly married couple and they were given every imaginable luxury. Gotama, however, increasingly became dissatisfied with his opulent lifestyle. At the age of 29, Gotama's wife bore him a son whom he named Rāhula, meaning 'chain'. Could it have been that Gotama was feeling chained to the palace? By all accounts he felt an increasing 'dis-ease' with life and wanted to find out what lay outside the palace. Certainly, living a life of pleasure is seen as *the sixth act of a Buddha.*

One day Gotama explored further away from the palace than normal and came across an old man with grey hair who was bent double. On the next trip out with his chariot driver he came across a man desperately ill. On his next trip he came across a corpse being carried to a funeral pyre. The final sight was of a wandering ascetic who had nothing yet looked supremely contented and at ease with himself. This final sighting gave Gotama the idea of leaving home and finding out the answer to his question of why there is suffering. There are legends which maintain it was the gods who appeared to Gotama on these four sightings, and that they muffled the sounds of his horse so that they were not heard on his final departure from the palace. The legend says Gotama took a last look at his sleeping son and then ordered Channa, his chariot driver, to take him away from the palace and then return home without him.

Gotama was now a mendicant, or *samaṇa*; this great renunciation of the pleasures of the world is *the seventh act of a Buddha.* He studied under two great meditation teachers, one after the other, and from them learned various forms of yoga and other meditative techniques. Indeed, Gotama became so accomplished in meditation that his teachers invited him to take over from them. At this point in history it was quite common for men—and indeed women as well—to 'go forth', to give up their responsibilities as family members and become homeless. The purpose of these world-renouncers was to strive after truth through various means—thinking and discussing ideas with others, meditation, ascetic practice, and the practice of yoga.

Three kinds of activity seemed to have preoccupied these wandering seekers after truth. First, the practice of austerity, including enduring discomfort, undertaking vows to live like a cow, fasting, and going around naked. Second, the cultivation of meditative or contemplative techniques which produced altered states of consciousness. This was understood to bring the practitioner to a deeper sense of knowledge and understanding of the world. Third, there was the discussion and development of various philosophical views. Some wandering seekers practised all three of the above disciplines, others focused on one or two.

These wandering ascetics (*samaṇas*) were counter-cultural. They were independent and did not buy into the Brahmanic world view. This meant that they offered a rival vision of society which was a threat to the Brahmanic tradition. New Religious Movements often threaten the established order, as they offer teachings and practices which are more relevant to the felt needs and aspirations of society. Sometimes, however, ideas from new movements can be absorbed into the dominant tradition. Indeed, Rupert Gethin (1998:15) suggests that some of the ideas taught by the wandering ascetics became a part of the Brahmanic teaching. Examples of this assimilation include 'philosophical views about the ultimate nature of man and his relationship to the universe at large'.

Of course, Gotama's upbringing took place a long way away from Vedic civilisation. Writing about the one who was to become the Buddha, Gombrich (1988:49) comments:

> Certainly, when he walked southeast into central Bihar, the scene of his enlightenment, he encountered brahminical culture with the critical eye of someone who had not been brought up to take its presuppositions for granted.

Gotama's quest for enlightenment

For six years, Gotama put all his efforts into trying to gain insight into the cause of suffering and how it may be eliminated. Having moved around from teacher to teacher he was now associated with five other ascetics. On one occasion he undertook a 49 day fast but enlightenment still proved elusive. These ascetic practices constitute *the eighth stage of a Buddha*. Gotama, now 35, had experienced both luxury and asceticism in their extremes but still had not found an antidote to suffering. Could there be a middle way? Might the answer lie between the two extremes of luxury and asceticism? Gotama was now all by himself having been abandoned by his five fellow ascetics who had looked to him as a leader. He sat under a fig tree[2] and vowed not to move until he was enlightened. He began to meditate, and stayed there for some time between three days to eight weeks.

There are a number of accounts of Gotama's activities under the tree of enlightenment in which Māra, the opposer of Gotama's quest, features prominently. A fairly standard Buddhist answer to the question of who or what is Māra is that Māra is a term for death or the temptation to do wrong. Māra is seen as the symbol of all unskilful behaviour that prevents progress to enlightenment, an impersonal and destructive force and influence. Another possible understanding is that Māra is a giant.[3] J. W. Boyd (1975:165) comments that 'Māra' comes from the Pali root *mārayati*, meaning 'that which kills,' and that death here refers not only to an individual's passing

---

[2] Often known as the 'bodhi' tree, from the Sanskrit meaning 'enlightment.'

[3] Sanskit: *yak*; the related word in Pali, *yakkha*, means a 'troublesome spirit'.

away but also to the continual process of birth, growing old, becoming sick and dying. Ling (1997:61) reminds us that the intention of Māra is to blind people to the true nature of reality, and points out that this activity is expressed by one of his titles, the 'Dark One'. J. W. Boyd (1975:165) agrees when he says that Māra is associated with 'smokiness and murkiness'.

Māra exists at the edge of the sixth and highest heaven of the sense-desire realm but could not quite reach the next level up, the realm of pure form.[4] In the realm of sense-desire, the inhabitants understand the world in terms of what is desirable or undesirable, whereas the *brahma* gods of the pure form realms have a more subtle understanding of existence. Harvey (2001:85) says that Māra is 'not just a name for just one being, but for a kind of being. Like all gods, a *māra* will eventually die, but his position will be later taken over by another *māra*, another being who has fallen into the same trap, and who seeks to entrap others.'

The gods who watched the tree of enlightenment in anticipation of Gotama's breakthrough fled at the sight of Māra on his elephant accompanied by his armies of 'desire, aversion, hunger and thirst, craving, tiredness and sleepiness, fear and doubt'. (Gethin, 1998:23) The next dark onslaught was the arrival of the three attractive daughters of Māra. On failing to seduce Gotama by their beauty, they disappeared into the ground. Māra then sent floods and storms to deflect Gotama from his quest for Enlightenment. This was unsuccessful and, as a last resort, Māra spoke of his merit and the witnesses he

---

[4] The six heavens or *realms of desire* are referred to as Naraka, Preta, Tiryagyoni, Manuṣya, Asura and Deva realms. Above this, there are 16 *pure form realms*, where beings have capacity for sight, hearing and consciousness. Finally, there are four *formless realms*. There is no form or body in existence in these realms; they are only mental states. All in all, there are 26 realms or heavens.

could call upon to testify to his moral achievements. He then challenged Gotama as to what evidence he could muster to vouch for his spiritual practice. At this point Gotama touched the ground with his right hand, calling on the earth itself to witness to the meritorious deeds he carried out in previous lives and his worthiness to be enlightened. The iconic earth-touching *mudrā* (gesture made with the hands) signalled the conquest of Māra and the enlightenment of Gotama. Terwiel (1994:155) recounts the appearance at this point of Mother Thorani, whose name is derived from the Sanskrit *dharani* meaning 'earth, soil or ground'. Mother Thorani appeared as a beautiful young lady, a personification of the ground beneath Gotama.

> She testified for the Buddha [to-be] by wringing from her tresses of hair the amount of water that had flowed from pouring water after meritorious deeds in [the] Buddha's past existences. The amount of water was so immense that Māra's army was drowned in it.[5]

Some Buddhists, particularly western Buddhists, view the narrative of Māra's temptations as the externalisation of Gotama's inner conflicts in his intense journey to discover the solution to suffering. Other Buddhists will take a much more literal view of Māra's activities and view the attacks on the Buddha-to-be as a showdown between cosmic powers.

---

[5] This deity is encountered in the ritual of building a house. Thorani appears a second time when, as a personification of the ground, she opens up and swallows Devadatta, the evil cousin of the Buddha who wished to create schism in the *saṅgha* (community of monks) and kill the Buddha. Thus, a ceremony of appeasement to Mother Thorani, may be carried out when something happens to a person such as a polluting or unlucky event.

Some Christians may believe that Gotama was deluded by his significantly altered state of consciousness as a result of intense, sustained mental focus. This, they may suggest, was caused by being removed from rational ways of processing information. Others may believe that Gotama's lack of openness to God may have prevented him from discovering God. I dare say that some Christians would go further and suggest that the devil prevented Gotama from experiencing or understanding God but permitted him to understand some truth: that desire is the cause of our suffering, and that the letting-go of desires and attachments is the way to be liberated from our suffering.

On the other hand, could it be possible that the devil did *not* wish Gotama to discover a pathway which, if followed, would lead people to be less selfish and more compassionate? The soon-to-be-enlightened Gotama and his followers would shortly teach the Five Precepts and the Eight Fold Path. To commit to these teachings would involve followers, both as individuals and as part of like-minded communities, living out values similar to those taught by Jesus some 450 years later, such as those in the Sermon on the Mount. I accept that they would be kingdom values without Christ the king, but living selflessly is surely a God-pleasing way to live.

Gotama's conquest of Māra reflects *the ninth act of a Buddha.*

The Buddha's enlightenment

Gotama, in his first stage of meditation, began to understand his previous existences. He was also able to recall 91 eons of time, measuring reincarnations of universes. In his second stage of meditation, he discovered that every element of the universe—including our lives—is in a state of constant flux. Here, Gotama is moving away from Hindu concepts of personhood and the abiding of the soul. In the third stage, Gotama realised that he had overcome his cravings and ignorance. He achieved *nibbāna* or enlightenment. This included gaining insight into the true nature of the cosmos and this was later explained as The Four Noble Truths, these are:

- First, the fact that we all experience suffering, dis-ease, 'unsatisfactoryness' (*dukkha*).

- Second, the origin of this suffering or lack of satisfaction comes from our craving and striving (*taṅhā*).

- Third, that we can cease our suffering by stopping our craving.

- Fourth, the way leading to the cessation of suffering/enlightenment lies at the end of following the *Magga*, the Middle Way, also known as the Eight-Fold Path.

This act of attaining enlightenment and buddhahood is *the tenth act of a Buddha*. According to Buddhist teaching, the Buddha achieved his quest for enlightenment at Bodh Gaya. He remained there for a period of up to seven weeks considering what he might do next: it is said that he felt that what he discovered would be too hard for others, even seekers after truth, to understand. In the *Majjhima Nikāya* (Carus, 1994b:also cited by)[44], there is an account of the Great (Mahā) Brahmā Sahampati coming to the Buddha and requesting him to preach:

> Alas! the world must perish, should not the Holy One, the Tathāgata, decide not to teach the

Dharma. Be merciful to those that struggle; have compassion upon the sufferers; pity the creatures who are hopelessly entangled in the snares of sorrow. There are some beings that are almost free from the dust of worldliness. If they hear not the doctrine preached, they will be lost. But if they hear it, they will believe and be saved. The Blessed One, full of compassion, looked with the eye of a Buddha upon all sentient creatures, and he saw among them beings whose minds were but scarcely covered by the dust of worldliness, who were of good disposition and easy to instruct. He saw some who were conscious of the dangers of lust and wrong doing.

And the Blessed One said to Brahmā Sahampati: 'Wide open be the door of immortality to all who have ears to hear. May they receive the *Dharma* by faith.'

The teaching of the Buddha

This constitutes the eleventh and penultimate act of the Buddha. The Buddha's teaching spanned 45 years. His teaching began after his enlightenment, when he taught some of the truths he discovered by himself to his five former companions, who were still searching for enlightenment.

His first sermon is referred to as the 'Setting in Motion the Wheel of Truth' (*Dhamma Cakka Pavattana Sutta*). In this sermon, the Buddha gave an exposition of what we refer to as the Four Noble Truths. Some believe that the Buddha was following a contemporary medical model—indicating what the sickness was (in this case, suffering), its cause (thirst, striving and clinging), that it was curable (get rid of desire and suffering will cease), and then prescribing the treatment—following the Noble Eightfold Path.

The First Noble Truth, known as *dukkha*, 'suffering', posits the view that sentient forms of life experience a measure of pain, both physical and emotional. It may vary from a sense of something missing from our lives or a sense of dissatisfaction, to profound emotional and/or physical suffering. We have to leave those we love; we have to engage with those we do not like; we have to do what we do not wish to do, and we cannot achieve all that we attempt. This truth points to the reality that to be alive means to experience suffering in various ways and to varying degrees.

The Second Noble Truth, known as *samudaya*, 'origin', identifies the cause or origin of suffering: suffering derives from a craving or thirst (*taṅhā*) for pleasure, or hanging on to that which gives us satisfaction. Three types of craving are identified in the Buddha's first sermon: there is the craving for sensual pleasure; then there is the craving for existence—which ranges from, for example, putting all our efforts into preserving our ego or careers, all the way to not being able to let go of life when death approaches. And lastly, there is the craving after non-existence—the desire to get rid of or escape from stressful situations and people we do not get on with. Harvey (1990:53) reminds us of two other forms of behaviour which cause suffering: the practice of adhering to particular views and asserting their correctness, often in a dogmatic manner, which usually creates unpleasant situations and restricts our growth and development; and the belief in a 'self', leads to selfish and harmful behaviour.

The Third Noble Truth, *nibbāna*, is that the cessation of suffering is brought about by a quenching of thirst, or a letting go of our desires. Even the desire to be liberated from suffering has to be transcended before a true understanding of reality can be experienced. This experience would be the beginning of extinguishing the fires of greed, hatred and delusion, the state referred to as enlightenment or *nirvāṇa* (Sanskrit; Pali *nibbāna*). This is not the best place for a discussion of enlightenment, as each Buddhist tradition has its own understanding of the nature of enlightenment and how it is reached; we will examine the paths to enlightenment in the appendix.

The Fourth Noble Truth, *magga*, is the way that leads to the cessation of suffering. This is a middle way which avoids the extremes of pleasure seeking and various forms of ascetic practice. The path has eight training components to it, which is why it is referred to as the Eightfold Path. The path has three foci: wisdom, morality, and mind development. The first two training components are right view or understanding and right thought—which corresponds to wisdom. Right speech, right action, right livelihood relate to morality. Mind development consists of right effort, right mindfulness, and right concentration.

As the path is followed, the unwholesome qualities of greed, hatred and delusion fall away and the wholesome qualities of non-attachment, loving-kindness and wisdom emerge. Following the path brings peace and a significant reduction in suffering, as we learn to respond appropriately to the way the world actually is. Ultimately, as the path is followed at a higher level, the Buddhist achieves enlightenment, or complete liberation from suffering.

An important Buddhist teaching, and one that is related to the Four Noble Truths, is 'conditioned arising' or 'dependent origination'. This is the understanding that all things come into being because of certain conditions. Nothing is independent in our conditioned world; if something exists, it has arisen because of certain preconditions. Once these conditions cease, then that thing—whether it be a thought, an action or a person—will no longer exist. Thus, we read in the *Saṃyutta Nikāya* 2:28, 'That being, this comes to be; from the arising of that, this arises; that being absent, this is not; from the cessation of that, this ceases.'

Suffering is one of the three marks of conditioned phenomena. The other two marks are non-self (*anatta*) and impermanence (*anicca*). We are constantly changing, and so any belief that we can find a permanent fulfilment in people, positions, possessions or achievements—all of which are also constantly changing—simply creates suffering. The teaching of the Buddha then points us in the direction of liberation from sufferings.

The Buddha invited those who were interested to follow him. It was an invitation to leave home and family and to put into practice the teachings of the Buddha with a view to seeing if those teachings were effective. As the number of followers grew, a monastic code emerged; these rules are recited by monastics on a regular basis, and confession is made if these rules are broken. In time, an order of nuns was established, beginning with the Buddha's step-mother who was the first ordained nun.

The Buddha was a creative and skilful teacher. Through discernment and questioning, he was able to establish where his questioner was at, and offer an appropriate answer. This capacity for communicating by skilful means is referred to as *upāya*. The Buddha also had the ability to engage easily with people from all walks of life. These factors, along with the invitation to put into practice his teachings to see if they actually worked, were reasons why the Buddha's teachings were readily accepted.

The *parinibbāna* of the Buddha

At the age of 80 the Buddha become unwell with food poisoning. He continued for three months to wander around, controlling his pain through meditation. In the *Mahā Parinibbāna Sutta*, we read that the Buddha said to his attendant:

> I am frail, Ānanda, old, aged, far gone in years. This is my eightieth year, and my life is spent. Even as an old cart, Ānanda, is held together with much difficulty, so the body of the Tathāgata is kept going only with supports. (*Mahā Parinibbāna Sutta* 2:32)

Māra continued to tempt the Buddha by inviting him to pass away before he was ready to do so. The Buddha indicated that he would pass into final *nibbāna* at a point of his own choosing, and indicated that it would be in three months' time. This renouncing of the Buddha's will to live was accompanied with a powerful earthquake and thunder. (*Last Days of the Buddha* 1998:33)

Ānanda, who at this stage was not enlightened, was overcome by emotion as he began to prepare a final resting place for the Buddha in the Sala Grove near Kusinārā. He went to the door of the monks' dwelling place and began to weep but the Buddha called for him and said:

Enough, Ānanda, do not sorrow, do not lament. For have I not taught from the very beginning that with all that is dear and beloved there must be change, separation, and severance? Of that which is born, come into being, compounded, and subject to decay, how can one say: 'May it not come into dissolution!'? There can be no such state of things. (3:58)

Even at the very last stages of his life, the Buddha was still willing to expound the *Dhamma*, his teachings and methods. The story is told of Subhadda, a wandering ascetic, who asked if other teachers had achieved enlightenment. In response, the Buddha did not criticize other systems, but indicated that the key feature of true teaching was the Eightfold Path. It was this which led the way to enlightenment. This was not part of any teaching that Subhadda had come across before, and after the Buddha explained the *Dhamma* to him, Subhadda took refuge in the Buddha, the *Dhamma* and the *saṅgha* (the Buddhist community) and was admitted into the community of monks.

The Buddha asked his monks if they had any questions they wished to ask before he passed away. On ascertaining that there were no questions, he said to those gathered, 'All conditioned things are subject to change. Attain perfection through diligence!' (*Dīgha Nikāya* II.156). He then passed over from this world to a final *nibbāna*—a state of enlightenment without physical conditions attached. This final passing or *parinibbāna* happened whilst the Buddha was in the highest realm of mental state, a state of neither perception nor non-perception. Passing into final *nibbāna* is *the twelfth and final act of a Buddha.*

The Buddha issued clear instructions as to what should be done with his remains. They were to be treated like those of an emperor, wrapped in cloth, placed in a coffin and cremated. They were then to be placed in a memorial (*stūpa*) at a place where four roads meet. This does not sound like the words of a man who had renounced all attachments! The Buddha, however, understood the affection and esteem in which he was held by his followers and knew that left to them there would have been the most elaborate of cremation ceremonies! True, the Buddha had renounced his worldly status but his followers had not forgotten that he was the son of the ruler of the Shākya clan. In addition, he was viewed by his followers as the king of the *Dhamma*, its discoverer and supreme teacher. The Buddha wished his followers to mark his final passing into *nibbāna* in an appropriate but not lavish manner. The idea of a *stūpa* where four roads meet was to position the memorial in an accessible location for his followers to come to pay their respects. In fact, the chief Brahmin officiating at the cremation of the Buddha distributed the relics to eight groups of people, while the ashes of the cremation fire and the bowl used to distribute the relics were given to two further groups.

In a conversation with Ānanda, the Buddha had indicated that he had "taught the *Dhamma* without holding anything back", and that the *saṅgha* depended on the *Dhamma*, not on any leader, even himself. Members of the *saṅgha* should look to their own self-reliant practice, with the clearly taught *Dhamma* as guide: with themselves and the *Dhamma* as 'island' and 'refuge'." (*Dīgha Nikāya* 11.100, quoted by Harvey, 1990:26) Indeed, the Buddha specified that after his *parinibbāna*, the monastic community should take both the *Dhamma* and the *Vinaya* (a code of monastic disciplines) as their teachers.

For the Buddhist, the Buddha is seen as one who has transcended the countless cycles of rebirth and consequent suffering through the achievement of enlightenment. The cause of suffering and its cure was found by the Buddha in his discovery of the *Dhamma*, the Truth of all things, which had been lost from our world. The category of a Buddha does not fit into our western categories of human or divine: Buddhahood is a category all by itself. A Buddha is one who has extinguished the fires of greed, hatred and delusion, and who lives out the four qualities of loving kindness, compassion, joy at the happiness and success of others, and even-handedness.

We have looked at the key aspects of the one who became known as the Buddha, and now turn to the life of Jesus Christ.

The Life Of Christ In 12 Acts

The '12 acts' is a helpful rubric by which to understand the Buddha's life. As we read these acts, we gain an overview of his life. I have also selected 12 aspects from Christ's ministry, starting with his eternal nature and the predictions of his birth, and finishing with his return to this world. These acts may serve as an introduction to the life of Christ for the Buddhist. There is some equivalence between the acts of the Buddha and the acts of Christ; for example, the birth narratives of both are mentioned, both births are attested by cosmic signs, and there are the predictions of an old man in both birth narratives. Although there may well have been a Buddhist community in Egypt around the time of the birth of Christ, I am not suggesting that some borrowing between the two traditions has taken place. My motivation in doing this is to communicate the life of Jesus to Buddhists using this framework of 12 acts. As you read through this section, ask yourself "in what ways could the 12 acts of Christ best be communicated to the Buddhists you know–by painting, drama or cartoon?"

The pre-existence of Christ

We read that Jesus Christ, the divine *Logos*, was with God in the beginning and, in fact, is God. (John 1:1) The Christian Scriptures contain the prediction or prophecy that the Son of God would take on human form and be known as Jesus Christ. Jesus is the Greek form of *Yeshua*, which comes from a Hebrew verb meaning 'to save'. Jesus then is a personal name, while Christ is a title meaning 'anointed' (from the Greek *Christos*)— in this case, anointed or appointed by God to be the saviour, or the intermediary figure between God and humanity. Certainly Jesus claimed to be the Son of God, maintaining that God was his Father. Elsewhere (John 17:5), Jesus mentions the glory he had with the Father before the world was created, and that he 'and the Father are one'. (John 10:30) The following predictions or prophecies indicate that a divine plan was worked out and, in God's time, came to pass. (see Galatians 4:4) Christ's mother Mary would be a virgin (Isaiah 7:14), the birth would take place in Bethlehem, and Christ would be born into the tribe of Judah. (Micah 5:2 and see also Genesis 49:10)

There is an indication that God's son would be called out of Egypt (Hosea 11:1), and we read in Matthew 2:13-14 that Christ and his parents escaped to Egypt when Herod ordered the death of all male children under two years of age in and around Bethlehem. This was an effort to get rid of the Christ who was referred to as king of the Jews by the wise men who had followed the star. After Herod's death, an angel appeared in a dream to Joseph and instructed him to leave Egypt with Mary and Jesus and return home. (Matthew 2:19-20) It was predicted that Jesus Christ would die for humanity (Isaiah 53:4-6) and that at his death soldiers would gamble for his clothes. (Psalm 27:35) Christ's final words from the cross were also anticipated. (Psalm 22:1)

The conception of Jesus

The Bible tells of God sending the angel Gabriel to Mary, a virgin who was engaged to Joseph, a descendant of King David. He announced that this young teenager had found favour with God and that she would give birth to a son who was to be named Jesus. In response to her question 'how will that happen?' the angel replies 'The Holy Spirit will come upon you, and the power of the most high will overshadow you. So the holy one to be born will be called the Son of God.' (Luke 1:35)

The birth of Christ

It is interesting to note that the birth narrative of Christ involves a group from the margins of Jewish society and a group from outside the country. The good news of Christ's birth is announced to shepherds as they are out working at night. They are informed about the birthplace of Jesus (Bethlehem), and given a description of what the child will be wearing (cloth strips) and where he will be lying (a cattle feeding trough). The shepherds went to Bethlehem and, after seeing the child, began to tell others about the event. Shepherding was considered a very lowly occupation in the region at that time, and shepherds were not generally considered trustworthy by the rest of society.

The second group of people were the *magi*, or wise men. These astrologers/astronomers believed that significant appearances in the sky pointed to important events on earth. As wise men, they interpreted the night sky and both their own dreams and the dreams of others, and they applied those interpretations to what they saw around them. It may have been that they had a special interest in Judaism, given that 500 years earlier a Jew had saved their ancestors and was placed in charge of all the wise men of Babylon—in the Old Testament, we read that Daniel said to King Nebuchadnezzar of Babylon,

> 'The great God has shown the king what will take place in the future. The dream is true and the interpretation is trustworthy.'
>
> Then King Nebuchadnezzar fell prostrate before Daniel and paid him honour saying 'Surely your God is the God of gods and the Lord of kings and a revealer of mysteries for you were able to reveal this mystery.' (Daniel 2:46-47)

Daniel is then tasked to oversee the work of the wise men who were retained by the palace.

These wise men who came to pay homage to Christ could be the fulfilment of an Old Testament prophecy concerning Christ, that 'nations will come to your light and kings to the brightness of your dawn.' (Isaiah: 60:3) After a conversation with a troubled Herod, the wise men saw the guiding star again and were overjoyed when it led them to the new-born king of the Jews. They bowed down and worshipped Christ the king, opening their treasures and presenting Christ with kingly gifts: presents of gold, incense and myrrh. It may well that these gifts were used to provide for the family during their time of exile in Egypt.

There are two accounts of Christ being identified as a saviour on the occasion of his dedication to God at the temple in Jerusalem. The occasion marked the purification of his mother Mary; forty days had passed since she had given birth, meaning she was now ritually clean and able to visit the temple in Jerusalem, some five miles away from where Christ was born in Bethlehem. The other reason for the visit to the temple was to dedicate Jesus, the first born son, to God. We read that God had revealed to Simeon, a devout old man, that before he passed away he would see Christ, the Son of God. Experiencing a divine urge from God, Simeon went into the temple courts and, meeting Mary and Joseph, took Jesus in his arms and praised God saying:

> Sovereign Lord as you have promised, you now dismiss your servant in peace. For my eyes have seen your salvation [the child Jesus] which you have prepared in the sight of all people, a light for revelation to the Gentiles and for glory to your people Israel. (Luke 2:29-32)

Simeon went on to address Jesus' mother by saying:

> This child is destined to cause the falling and rising of many in Israel, and to be a sign that will be spoken against, so that the thoughts of many hearts will be revealed. And a sword will pierce your own soul too. (Luke 2:34-35)

The early life of Christ

The Christian Scriptures are virtually silent on the early life of Jesus. There is a snapshot of him aged 12 in Jerusalem: his parents left Jerusalem after the Feast of the Passover, probably travelling home to Nazareth with others from the village. His parents naturally assumed that he was with relatives or friends in another group nearby. The story is recounted in Luke 2:41-52, and tells us that after a day of travelling, when his parents look for Jesus they could not find him. They returned to Jerusalem and, after three days, eventually located him in the temple. There he was listening to the teachers and asking them perceptive questions. 'Everyone who heard him was amazed at his understanding and his answers.' (Luke 2:47) In Mark 6:3 we read that when the people of Nazareth heard him teach in the synagogue, they were amazed both by his teaching and miracles. They wanted to know where his wisdom came from—after all, was he not a local carpenter, was his mother not Mary, were not his four brothers and sisters in the village? There is no reference here to Joseph, his legal father, and this may be because he had already passed away, in which case it is only natural to assume that Jesus, as the oldest son, continued the family's carpentry business. My point here is simply that Jesus was understood to be a tradesman, rooted in the local community.

Some may see some correlation between Jesus as a boy in the temple conversing with the teachers and Gotama as a seven year old boy meditating while waiting for his father who was officiating at a ploughing ceremony. We read that Gotama's father was looking for his son and eventually found him under a tree in a deep meditative state. The tree cast no shadow indicating that the sun was directly overhead; it was, however, later in the afternoon. This apparent ability to make time stand still indicated that the Buddha-to-be had unusual powers. In both cases the sons were lost and were found to be exhibiting supernatural abilities.

The baptism of Jesus

The beginning of Jesus' public ministry was signified by his baptism by John. In this act of baptism, he identifies with those he had come to save, and he behaves as a God-honouring Jewish male would have acted. Jesus expresses commitment to God and to the coming of His kingdom. It may well be that some Pharisees from Jerusalem who were checking up on John's activities may have looked at Jesus' act of baptism and privately wondered what sinful act this young man was repenting of. It is interesting to note that as soon as Jesus was baptised in the River Jordan he went up out of the water. This is in contrast to the people who were baptised yet who remained in the river, confessing their sins to John, who would offer advice on living a better life. (Luke 3:11-14) It is at his baptism that Jesus experiences special affirmation from the other two persons of the Trinity: the Holy Spirit and the Father.

The temptation of Christ (Matthew 4:1 - 11, Mark 1:12 - 13 and Luke 4:1 - 13)

In the account of the enlightenment of the Buddha we saw how dark forces challenged his quest to break through to a state of awareness of truth. Shortly after his baptism, Jesus was led by the Holy Spirit into the wilderness for 40 days, and during that time he was tempted by the devil. The text indicates that all of this was brought about by God. The purpose was not only to defeat the devil, but to test his Son and develop the divine relationship—Father, Son and Spirit—in the context of what can only be described as intense spiritual conflict. There is a parallel here between the temptation of Adam who gave in to Satan, chose to disobey God and fractured his relationship with the divine. In contrast, Christ triumphed over Satan and demonstrated his ongoing commitment to the redemptive task that was becoming increasingly clear to him.

In his first temptation, Christ was tempted to use his own power to turn stones into bread and satisfy the hunger he was experiencing due to his fast. That would have meant him working in isolation from God the Father and the Holy Spirit who had led him into the wilderness. The second temptation was for Christ to demonstrate his supernatural power by throwing himself off the highest point of the temple and allowing the angels to catch him. What would be served by such an action? Often in Scripture, the demonstration of power (known as a power encounter) serves to prove divinity and thereby challenge and change the commitment of the audience. The devil had already acknowledged the divinity of Christ, and understood how Christ's divinity was a threat to the power that the devil exercised over humanity at that time. The third temptation for Christ was for the devil to withdraw his world dominion and return it to Christ, the rightful owner. This would be done if Christ would but worship the devil. True, Christ came to reconcile this world to the Father and restore it to its original purpose, but he also came to gain complete dominion over the devil. These temptations were not subtle and we can see the devil's attempt to divert the Son of God from his redemptive quest.

The calling of Christ's disciples and the establishing of early Christian communities

There were many who accepted Jesus as their teacher. However, he referred to his group of 12 male followers as his 'disciples'; sometimes the term used is 'apostles', meaning 'sent ones'. Christ invested the three years of his public ministry in teaching and training them so that they would continue to do the things he had taught them after he physically left this earth.

In Jewish culture at that time there were many teachers (rabbis) with their own groups of disciples. The accepted practice was for a young man to approach a rabbi and ask if he may become a disciple. A disciple would carry out any necessary tasks for the rabbi, and in return would receive a theological education. Well-known rabbis would be highly selective as to who they accepted as disciples. Jesus broke with that practice and called people to follow him; this put him at a risk of losing face should his offer be rejected. Rabbinic groups or schools normally had a peaceful atmosphere for acquiring knowledge. In contrast, Jesus' disciples were high on adventure and low on security, and they were certainly dependent on the giving of their supporters. They were also frequently harassed by some of the teachers of the Law. Jesus was their rabbi and elder brother, God was their Father, but they had to learn to accept other followers of Christ as family members.

This was a community who heard the secrets of the kingdom of God, questioned Jesus about it, and tried to put into practice what they learnt. Yet as Collinson (2004:52) points out:

> This community did not exist for its own sake, but for the sake of others. While it provided support and encouragement, the lives of the disciples were to be focused outward towards serving others.

We see this outward focus as Jesus gives authority to the 12 disciples 'to drive out evil spirits and to heal every disease and sickness'. (Matthew 10:1) They were sent to the Jewish people to let them know that the kingdom of God was near. After the ascension of Christ, the disciples continued his ministry and the Church expanded rapidly in Jerusalem and the surrounding areas. Within a fairly short period of time, the story of Jesus is told to non-Jews, in non-Jewish terms; those speaking to

Gentiles talk of the 'Lord Jesus' as opposed to "Jesus Christ', using the Greek word *Kyrios* ('Lord') rather than the Greek word *Kristos*, a translation of the Jewish term 'messiah'. (Acts 11:19–21

At one level we may say that the Church is brought into being through the witness of the first disciples who were trained and sent out. This may have some resonance with the initial formation of the Buddhist *saṅgha*, where the five ascetics who had practised with the Buddha before his enlightenment became enlightened themselves, and shortly afterwards, there was a total of 60 monks who had become fully enlightened, or *arhat*s. The Buddha then sent out these disciples/monks to spread the *Dhamma* and commissioned them as follows:

> Walk, monks, on tour for the blessing of the many folk, for the happiness of the many folk, out of compassion for the world, for the welfare, the blessing, the happiness of the gods and humans. (Vinaya 1.21)

Later, some monks asked the Buddha if they could wear boots as walking barefoot over difficult terrain from village to village was very time-consuming. The Buddha refused to give them permission, saying that if the monks wore boots, while they would certainly make good progress, they would be perceived as soldiers by the villagers. Christ sent his early disciples out two by two with the most basic of supplies and they were to be reliant on the hospitality offered to them by the people of the villages they visited. Being vulnerable in the communities in which we work could, counter-intuitively, increase our safety and enhance the openness of people to what we say.

The teaching and healing ministry of Christ

Unlike the Buddha, Christ spent a very short period as a teacher in public ministry—only three years. These years were spent as an itinerant teacher who preached and healed the sick, including exorcising those possessed by evil spirits. During this time he had a strong focus on mentoring the twelve men who travelled with him and who he would commission to make disciples of others after his ascension into heaven.

The ministry of Jesus was characterised by authoritative teaching and we read of the amazement of his large audiences at his wisdom. (See, for example, Mark 6:2.) Matthew 7:28-29 speaks of the crowds being 'amazed at this teaching, because he taught as one who had authority, and not as their teachers of the law.' Jesus used parables or everyday stories to illustrate important truths about God, His kingdom, and the appropriate way to live in it. He also asked a lot of questions without supplying answers.[6] This had the effect of drawing people into the story, a story which sometimes functioned as a riddle. There was enough light in these stories for the seeker after truth to find guidance, while the more casual listener may not grasp the significance. These parables touched on a variety of topics such as the nature of God's kingdom, serving God and being rewarded, prayer, love for one's neighbour, humility and judgement.

There are around 25 instances in the gospel accounts of Jesus healing the sick. These vary from the exorcisms of those

---

[6] Note the number of questions Jesus asks in Mark 8:17-19. In Luke 5:22-23, Jesus asks a question to demonstrate to his audience that he knows what they are thinking. Then we see Jesus responding to the Pharisees' criticism by asking 'Have you never read what David did when he was hungry?' This is quite a humorous question as the Pharisees spent a great deal of time reading what we now refer to as the Old Testament.

possessed by evil spirits to the healing of the blind, dumb, deaf, crippled and victims of leprosy. On three occasions we read of Jesus bringing the dead back to life. (Matthew 9:18-26, Luke 7:11-16 and John 11:1-45) In addition, we read of nine non-healing miracles. These include Jesus walking on water, calming a storm on a lake, turning water into wine (his first miracle) and, on two occasions feeding crowds of people: 5000 people (Matthew 14:15-21) and 4000 people. (Matthew 15:32-39) These miracles had four basic purposes. (Jensen, 1969:101-2) First, they alleviated suffering and sorrow, thus indicating the compassion that God had for humankind. Second, this divine activity demonstrates that God was drawing near in a tangible way; the kingdom of God was expanding as dark forces were being challenged and pushed back. Third, these miracles authenticated the fact that God was with Jesus (John 3:2; Acts 2:22), and indeed that the Father is in Christ and Christ is in the Father. (John 10:38) This would have made it easier for some to believe that Jesus was from God, although others stubbornly refused to accept this, and even suggested that Christ's power was demonic. (Luke 11:15) A final purpose for the miracles was that they created audiences for Jesus to speak to about the kingdom of God.

The death of Christ

This is dealt with in some detail in chapters six and seven, where we examine the understanding that Christ suffers the penalty for our sins so that we may be declared 'not guilty'. This possibility of forgiveness removes barriers between humankind and God but also repairs fractured relationships between humans. In addition, we find strong evidence in the account of Christ's death for the destruction of the devil's power over humankind, and indeed the cosmos. Looking back at the life of Jesus Christ after some 50 years had passed, one of his disciples wrote that 'the reason the Son of God appeared was to destroy the devil's work'. (1 John 3:8)

The resurrection of Christ

The disciples believed that when God would return to establish His kingdom on earth, He would raise to life those who had lived good lives in order to be part of this new era. Clearly they expected Jesus being raised by God to be a central part of that coming kingdom. An amazing aspect of the resurrection of Jesus for his disciples was that it happened only three days after he was crucified. This would have spoken to them of the arriving of at least the beginning of God's new order, which could be seen in the resurrection body of Christ—a body that had the natural capacities of eating, drinking and communicating, yet a body that could also 'appear and disappear and come and go through locked doors'. (N. T. Wright, 2008:3) The coming alive of Jesus Christ is viewed by Christians as a demonstration of his power over death and the sinister forces which lead to his death. This is a proclamation to humanity and the unseen world of cosmic beings that Christ is a conqueror.

Christ's return to heaven: ascension (Mark 16:19, Luke 24:50-53 and Acts 1:6-11)

Scripture teaches that Jesus was taken up into the air while talking with his disciples and then concealed from their view by a cloud. We note in passing that the cloud both concealed God and, at the same time, reminded people of God's presence. As the disciples were gazing into the sky, two men dressed in white appeared and asked how long they would continue to look and went on to say, 'This same Jesus, who has been taken from you into heaven, will come back in the same way you have seen him go into heaven.' (Acts 1:11) Heaven is the space for God, supernatural beings and the spirits of those who have died believing in Christ. It is to this space that Christ now returns in his resurrected, glorified body. Yet at the same time, he is equally at home in our space, the earth, as he is in what we call heaven. Speaking of the early disciples, N. T. Wright (2008:3) comments:

> They 'believed' that 'heaven' and 'earth' are the two interlocking spheres of God's reality, and that the risen body of Jesus is the first (and so far the only) object which is fully at home in both and hence in either, anticipating the time when everything will be renewed and joined together.

Christ resides in heaven or 'God's space', but we remind ourselves that he is also present with us by his Spirit and it is in partnership with him that we participate in the life and mission of God on earth. This relates to the words spoken by Jesus in the ascension story: 'But you will receive power when the Holy Spirit comes upon you and you will be my witnesses in Jerusalem, and in all Judea and Samaria, and to the ends of the earth.' (Acts 1:8) Similarly, in the words of what we refer to as the 'Great Commission' in Matthew 28:19-20, those who participate in God's mission will enjoy Christ's provision of resources.

Christ's mission continues in our space, here in our world. He is present through his followers especially in their coming together in churches. Indeed, he has a special relationship with the Church, and prevents it from being overcome by dark forces. Two quotes from Paul's letter to the Christians in Ephesus are apposite here:

God has placed all things under his [Christ's] feet and appointed him to be head over everything for the church, which is his body, the fullness of him who fills everything in every way. (Ephesians 1:22-23)

Paul also writes:

His [God's] intent was that now, through the church, the manifold wisdom of God should be made known to the rulers and authorities in the heavenly realms. (Ephesians 3:10)

Paul is saying that Christ's power and presence fills the Church; it is a gift but it is also a goal, in the sense that we need to learn to live appropriately in the light of this reality. As the Church does this, it will demonstrate qualities of loving-kindness, service, unity and wisdom as well as sharing the 'words' of the gospel. At the same time, by God's strength, the Church punches far above its weight, confounding both supernatural beings and the human order.

But what on earth is happening in heaven? Christ functions as an advocate for those who trust in him. This could be interpreted as representing us to God should the devil accuse us of wrongdoing. The point is that we have a divine and authoritative advocate, and there is no need for some ancestor, saint or enlightened being to intervene on our behalf. Christ is also understood to ask the Father to provide for the needs of his followers. The writer of a letter to Jewish converts who were under great pressure discusses in detail the high priestly aspect of Christ's ministry in heaven, emphasizing the supremacy of Christ over a human high priest. For example, we read that Christ did not conduct priestly activities in some man-made temple but 'entered heaven itself, to appear for us in God's presence'. (Hebrews 9:24)

We note that prayer was a distinctive feature of Christ's life on earth (see, for example, Luke 5:16); it was a conversing with his Father, and it is hardly surprising that it continues in heaven. We read of Jesus praying for Simon Peter that his faith would not fail (Luke 22:31-32). While Peter did deny the Lord at his trial, he was restored and became a strong leader in the early Church; Jesus' prayer was answered. Then there is the astonishing 'high priestly prayer' of Jesus in John 17. Here, prior to his betrayal by Judas, Jesus prays to his Father for himself but mainly for his disciples and all those who would eventually come to faith. Interestingly, he prays that all believers would love each other and would have within them the love that the Father has for the Son. Ultimately, this prayer will also be answered.

Christ's return to this world (*parousia*)

There are a number of things that we know about the second coming, or *parousia*, of Christ. We know that it will be unexpected (Matthew 24:44); it will be high profile (Revelation 1:7), and that Christ will come in power and glory. (Matthew 24:30) It is through Christ that God the Father will reconcile all things to himself. (Colossians 1:19-20) At this point, heaven and earth will be brought together and Christ the reconciler, conqueror, bringer of justice, assessor of all actions, and comforter, will be the focal point of a new creation.

Heaven should not be viewed as a final destination or ultimate existence. The ultimate end point is for a new heaven and a new earth to be joined together. This enlarged space of a new heaven and a new earth constitute the location for a permanent utopian existence. It will be populated by all who one day will be renewed by Christ the redeemer. This existence will be what God intended for humanity; it will not be challenged by dark forces because these will have been comprehensively dealt with by Christ's death and resurrection. This renewed creation will draw upon all the good that has been done by humankind from basic acts of kindness, integrity in the work place, through to scientific discovery and innovations which have alleviated suffering.

This chapter has briefly looked at the context into which the Buddha grew up and taught. We have examined the 12 acts of the life of the Buddha—and which are applicable to any buddha. We also selected and briefly examined 12 aspects of the life of Christ. All of this could be used to make a comparison between these figures but any examination should carefully note the differences between the two teachers. Describing the life of Jesus using this framework of 12 acts may help a Buddhist gain an overview of the life of Christ.

The next chapter goes on to examine issues such as whether the Buddha pointed to key moral functions of God, and whether he also pointed towards the coming of Jesus Christ. We also explore what appropriate Christian attitudes to the Buddhist world might look like based on responses from Paul, Jeremiah, and Abraham towards non-believers.

Pause for reflection

1. Can you suggest other events from the life of Jesus Christ which might be a more appropriate comparison to the 12 acts of the Buddha?

Chapter 3

God And The Buddha

In Gotama's quest to find the cause of and cure for suffering, was there any discovery of God and His work in the world? Did, as some Christians in Asia claim, the Buddha point to Jesus as the next Buddha of our world? What are biblical attitudes to those of other faiths, particularly when religious images are involved? This chapter discusses these three issues.

Christians may well ask why Gotama's intense and prolonged search after truth did not result in him finding God. We read that the Buddha thought that those who trusted in a supreme being were abandoning their moral responsibilities. For example, the teacher Makkhali Gosāla, the leader of the Ajīvaka fraternity, stated that 'there is no question of a person attaining maturity of character by good deeds, vows, penances or a religious life.' (*Dīgha Nikāya* 1:54) He believed that humankind is a product of the will of god, and that eventually everyone would be saved, but their salvation was not related to their efforts. The Buddha thought that Makkhali Gosāla's teaching was toxic, as he believed it would result in people living in a morally irresponsible manner.

Perhaps the closest we come to what we consider to be a personal god in Buddhism is the Mahā (Great) Brahma,[1] who is morally perfect and has very great knowledge and power but is not omniscient or omnipotent. Mahā Brahma, chief of the Brahmas, resides in the lowest of the sixteen Pure Form realms. The Buddha viewed him as a glorious being but not as an all-powerful creator. The Mahā Brahma is subject to the law of *karma* and has not yet achieved buddhahood, so does not have the power or knowledge possessed by the Buddha. The Great Brahma, however, believes that he may be the creator of the world. Peter Harvey (2001:96) draws from Walshe's *Thus I Have Heard* and explains that there are times when some of the heavens end and become empty. After an extensive period of time, they re-appear and a being from another realm is reborn as a Great Brahma. Then, after a while, he becomes lonely and wishes for the presence of others. In time, other higher gods are reborn, due to their *karma*, into the first level of the pure form level and become the servants of the Great Brahma. The Great Brahma believes that he has created these beings and these undergods who serve him also believe this. In time, when they are reborn as humans and they develop the capacity to remember their previous existence, they teach that there is an eternal creator being in another realm.

Our discussion has shown that, according to Buddhist teaching, while a powerful spiritual being can create a world, no guarantees are made about what kind of a world will be created. Power gives the capacity to create, but a powerful being without enlightenment and moral greatness may create a world of suffering. It is easy for Buddhists to conclude that

---

[1] The *brahma*s are a class of high gods.

this world of suffering was created by a powerful being—but one lacking in goodness! They may well even conclude that it would be personally damaging to worship such a creator!

The Sri Lankan scholar-monk, Walpola Rahula (1967:52) comments that an immortal soul and God are conceived by humankind and clung to in weakness and desire and ignorance for consolation but we all have to take responsibility for our own suffering and work at our own liberation. He writes:

> The Buddha's teaching does not support this ignorance, weakness, fear and desire, but aims at making man enlightened by removing and destroying them, striking at their very root. According to Buddhism, our ideas of God and Soul are false and empty.

True, Buddhism is understood by many as being atheistic. On the other hand, Geoff Hunt, founder of the New Buddha Way, takes the view that 'neither theism nor atheism has anything to do with the Buddha's concern... Absolutely nowhere in the entire Tipitaka does the Buddha try to prove that God does not exist nor does he argue against any such proof' (Hunt, 2010:78). The Buddha simply points out the danger of being morally passive and blaming a creator for one's personal failures.

Did the Buddha point to aspects of God's work?

I want to suggest that the Buddha pointed to three aspects of Buddhist understanding which, for the purposes of dialogue, may also be viewed as aspects of God's moral work. First, *nirvāṇa*.[2] This speaks of salvation or liberation from a constant cycle of being born, growing old, becoming sick and then dying, only to be reborn and repeat the same dismal process. Present day Buddhists, and particularly those in materially comfortable situations, view rebirth as the opportunity to live on, perhaps having an even more pleasurable life than the present one. People in the Buddha's time, however, were beginning to move into larger centres of population where disease spread rapidly. In addition, there was a caste system which was legitimised by Bramanic teaching—not a problem for Bramins and those from the warrior class, but oppressive and marginalising if you happened to be an untouchable.

Nibbāna describes ultimate liberation but it also refers to being freed from anxiety; members of Santi Asoke, a new Buddhist movement in Thailand, use *nippan* (the Thai version of the Pali word *nibbāna*) to denote liberation from some kind of addiction or unwholesome conduct. During my time researching this movement, Asoke members often made comments like 'I am *nipan jak buri*' meaning 'I am free from smoking cigarettes'. Those who knew me at that time took a dim view of my reliance on strong coffee, which I drunk to keep me awake after a 3am start to the day. In their view the next step on my spiritual journey was to experience *nibbāna* from coffee! Christians could use '*nibbāna*' as a word to describe liberation from sin, suffering and the effects of the Fall which, one day, will become a reality through the redeeming and reconciling work of Jesus Christ.

The second aspect to which the Buddha pointed was *karma*, or moral cause-and-effect. This reminded the people of his day that ultimately justice would be done, and to think carefully before taking a particular course of action. Of course,

---

[2] Sanskrit; Pali *nibbāna*.

in Buddhism there is no lawgiver who will judge, rather the law of *karma* which is embedded in the universe and ensures that each intentional action has an appropriate positive or negative response. Is there not some congruence between the idea of *karma* and the fact that God will ultimately bring about justice?

The third aspect to which the Buddha pointed was the *Dharma*.[3] This is the Buddhist term for 'ultimate truth', and in the next chapter I compare it to the concept of an impersonal god. The *Dhamma* was what was discovered by the Buddha under the tree of enlightenment. I intend no disrespect to the Buddhist tradition by suggesting that the three cardinal doctrines of *nibbāna*, *karma* and *Dhamma* are also aspects of God's work. Is it not the case that these three doctrines correspond to liberation, justice and truth? From a Christian perspective these are all aspects of God's governing action. The Buddha's pointing towards these key aspects is now diagrammed.

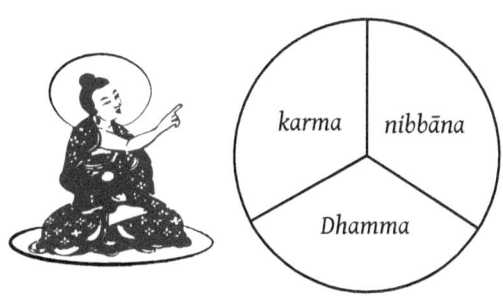

Figure 3.1: The Buddha's pointing to key 'aspects' of God's work

---

[3] Pal; Sanskrit *Dharma*.

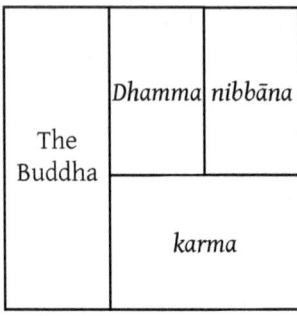

Figure 3.2: Buddhism after the passing of the Buddha

Another key question is why God did *not* allow himself to be discovered by the meditating Gotama, at least in ways that Christians recognise as being Christian? Had Gotama encountered God, then he would have taught about depending on God rather than about self-dependence. My conclusion is that this was neither the time nor the place for a non-Jew to experience God and teach about that experience. It was God's intention for Christ to be born some 400 years later in Israel. In terms of chronology we read that '[W]hen the time had fully come, God sent his Son, born of a woman, born under the law, to redeem those under the law, that we might receive the full rights of sons.' (Galatians 4:4) Some commentators, such as John Stott (1968:105), focus on how the conditions were particularly favourable for Christ to come and, in time, for the Gospel message to travel throughout the region, given the efficient and relatively safe network of roads created by the Roman military. The widespread use of the Greek language and possibly the readiness of many non-Jews to turn from the gods of Rome and Greece are also viewed as significant factors in the optimum timing of Christ's incarnation in history.

300 years prior to the enlightenment of Gotama, it had

been predicted that God's Son would be born among God's chosen people, the Jews. The Old Testament prophet Micah (5:2) said that the king they lived under was ineffective and that the only solution for inept kingship was for a new king to be born. This was predicted to take place not in Jerusalem, as it was corrupt, but rather in Bethlehem where the kingly line of David began. (R. Smith, 1984:44) Luke (2:4-7) records the birth of Jesus in Bethlehem. Micah (5:4) predicted that the new king 'will stand and shepherd his flock in the strength of the Lord, in the majesty of the name of the Lord his God'. Interestingly, Luke (2:8-20) recounts the appearance of an angel of the Lord to the shepherds who then went to Bethlehem to worship Christ, the new king, the good shepherd.

We may speculate that had the Buddha lived around 800 years later he may have encountered the gospel through the first Christians in India. Indeed, had he converted to Christianity, he may have become a great missionary of the Christian faith given his wisdom, capacity for clear teaching and charisma!

Did the Buddha predict the coming of Jesus Christ?

Each world has one Buddha at any time; it is said that no world could support the greatness of two Buddhas. The Buddha of this age is Gotama but the further we move away from his time on earth, the less his teachings will be put into practice, resulting in the increase of selfish and immoral behaviour. Peter Harvey (1990:67) notes that one commentary says:

> 5000 years after the *parinibbāna* (passing into *nibbāna* at death) of the Buddha, the practice of Buddhism will have disappeared, such that the period

of Gotama Buddha's influence will have ended. All his relics will then travel to the foot of the tree under which he attained enlightenment and disappear in a flash of light! This is referred to as the *parinibbāna* of the relics.

Extreme immoral behaviour then will lead to humankind's loss of the *Dhamma* and a new Buddha will be required to come and teach the Truth. The Buddhist tradition teaches that this will happen and that the next Buddha (currently a 10th stage bodhisattva) will be called Metteyya.[4] Many Theravadins hope that they will be reborn on this earth during Metteyya's time here and come to enlightenment under his tutelage. The following text from the *Mahāparinibbāna Sutta* (which may also be found in the work of Paul Carus (1994b:244-5)) is of interest, and features the words of the Historical Buddha:

> 'I am not the first Buddha who came upon earth, nor shall I be the last. In due time another Buddha will arise in the world, a Holy One, a supremely enlightened one, endowed with wisdom in conduct, auspicious, knowing the universe, an incomparable leader of men, a master of angels and mortals. He will proclaim a religious life, wholly perfect and pure; such as I now proclaim.' [At this point Ānanda asked the Buddha 'How shall we know him?'] The Buddha replied 'He will be known as Maitreya, which means he whose name is kindness'.

Dr Pracha Thaiwatcharamas, a Christian minister in NE Thailand, and a Laotian named Inta Chanthavongsouk both

---

[4] Pali; Sanskrit *Maitreya*, and also referred to as *Phra Sri Ariya* in Thai.

talk about Buddhist writings which may be understood to identify the coming Buddha with Christ. Chanthavongsouk (1999:25) cites Book 27, page 23, of the Thai Buddhist Scriptures.[5] Here, a Brahman discusses liberation in the Buddhist tradition with the Buddha. The Buddha tells him he should look for Maitreya and goes on to say:

> In the saviour who will come to save the world, you will see the puncture wounds like a wheel in the palms of his hands [and on] the bottom of his feet. In his side there is the mark of a stab wound and his forehead is full of scars. This God will be the big ark that will lead you to cross the cycle of birth and death to *nirvāṇa*. And you will find the three emerald Enlightened Ones [seen by some Christians as a reference to the trinity]. Do not prefer the old way.

Chanthavongsouk informs us that this was a well-known prophecy in the Buddhist village in which he grew up in Laos. The marks clearly refer to a prediction that as Jesus Christ hung on the cross he would have nails driven into his hands and feet, a sword thrust into his side, and marks on his head from the crown of thorns. In Buddhist tradition, a Buddha-to-be will be born with 32 marks; 31 representing the interconnected and transient abodes of *saṃsāra*[6] and one which represents the blissful state of *nibbāna*. Some of these marks are common to all beings who will become Buddhas in this rebirth; some of them point to the individual identity of the Buddha-to-be.

---

[5] There are 45 volumes; each volume represents one of the years that the Buddha taught the *Dhamma*.

[6] The impermanent, conditioned realms which exist outside *nibbāna*.

Thaiwatcharamas' account is fairly similar, and based on a document—allegedly a copy of Buddhist Scriptures—which had been given to his father. The document was written in the language of the old kingdom which was based in Chiang Mai, northern Siam; this may well refer to the Lanna kingdom which was established around the beginning of the 14th century. Thaiwatcharamas believes that these texts were not edited by Christians, as the document precedes the arrival of Christianity in Thailand (known as Siam up until 1939). The Roman Catholic missionary enterprise was well established in Siam by the 17th century, no doubt assisted by King Narai who reigned from Ayudhya from 1656 to 1688 and gave liberty for the preaching of the Christian faith.[7] The first resident Protestant missionaries arrived from America in 1833. Of course, it is possible that there were Chinese traders influenced by Nestorian Christianity in northern Siam prior to the arrival of Catholic missionaries, and for them to have talked about Christ being the Buddha of this age. This could have resulted in a Christian interpretation of certain well known Buddhist texts referring to Maitreya.

So far we have established that the next Buddha of our world will be named Maitreya, and that two Christians have come across documents which allegedly indicate that Maitreya will have marks on him which are in keeping with the injuries Christ sustained during his crucifixion. Some Christians believe that the 5000 year period mentioned at the beginning of this section is a translation error which should read 500 years. True, there is a passage in the *Cullavagga* (X:356) where the Buddha mentioned to his attendant the Venerable Ānanda, that the true *Dhamma* would last for only 500 years now that

---

[7] A concise history of mission in Thailand written by S Chumsriphan and P Pongudom et al., may be found in S.W. Sunquist, ed. (2001). *A Dictionary of Asian Christianity*. Cambridge: William B Eerdmans, pp.831-7.

women were going to be ordained as nuns, rather than the 1000 year period that it would have lasted if women were not ordained. The Buddha believed that having women in closer proximity with male monastics would be an extra distraction for monks, and would result in a more rapid dilution of the teaching of the *Dhamma*. It is true that 500 years does bring us up to the time of Christ, but far from dying out by that time, Buddhism continued to expand—so much for the idea that a new Buddha would be necessary to reintroduce Truth into the world! Could it be that the timeframe really is 5000 years, but the prophecy does not refer to the *first* coming of Christ to the earth, but rather to his *second* coming?

I have not yet been able to locate these passages mentioned by Thaiwatcharamas and Chanthavongsouk in the Thai Buddhist Canon. Equally, there is a lack of congruence between the self-dependence clearly taught by the Buddha and the Christian reliance on Christ to do for us what we cannot do for ourselves. I have mentioned this story to several Thai friends. In my experience, recent converts from Buddhism to Christianity are usually happy to believe that Christ's coming was predicted by the Buddha and that somehow Christ can be seen in the Buddhist tradition in which they were brought up. On the other hand, Buddhist monastic friends have not heard of the texts which refer to the marks on the coming Maitreya, and my suggestions about these gave them the impression that Christians have been misusing Buddhist Scriptures.

We have asked if the Buddha pointed to some of the moral aspects of God's work and if he predicted the coming of Jesus Christ, albeit as the next Buddha of this world! Let us now change topic and turn our attention to three characters from the Christian Scriptures and how they responded to people who did not worship their God. There may be lessons here for us as we work out how best to respond to Buddhists with their images, rituals, temples and very different worldview.

Formulating a Christian response to the Buddhist world - thoughts from Paul, Jeremiah and Abraham

Paul and the unknown god

In his sermon in Athens, around 52 CE, Paul looks at an earlier attempt of the Athenians to find a solution to the problem of their suffering (Acts 17:16-34). Shortly before the time of the Buddha, a plague struck Athens and the Athenians sacrificed to their many gods. This did not have the desired effect, and so they approached Epimenides, a Cretan philosopher and religious leader. He visited Athens and after seeing the plethora of religious images reasoned that there must be another god who was not represented by the images in the city but who, if called upon, would surely be good enough to act on their behalf. Epimenides suggested that if this unknown god was good and powerful, and if the citizens were to acknowledge their ignorance of him, then he would most likely stop the plague. He advised the people to release a flock of sheep on Mars Hill in Athens and whenever a sheep stopped grazing and laid down, it was slaughtered and offered up as a sacrifice, on that very spot, to the unknown god. According to Richardson (1981:C67-8), three Greek writers, Diogenes Laertius, Philostratus and Pausanias all write that the plague ceased. The Athenians continued to worship their many gods but added this unknown god, or indeed, some unknown gods to their pantheon of gods.

Like any devout Jew, Paul was extremely disturbed by idol worship. John Stott (1990:278) points out that the Greek verb *paroxyno* which translates 'greatly distressed' was a word used for a seizure or epileptic fit. Stott follows this up by commenting that *paroxyno* is a word that is regularly used in the Septuagint[8] to describe the Lord's anger, for instance at the creation of the golden calf at Mount Sinai. Paul could not escape the plethora of images; the word-picture here is one of a dense undergrowth or jungle of religious images. In fact, people of that era said that it was easier to find an idol than a person in Athens! Paul displays a jealousy for God's reputation, which surely gave an urgency to his preaching in the synagogue and his discussions with all who would engage with him in the *agora*, the market place, which was also the key location for discussing news and ideas. It may be helpful at this point to read Acts 17:16-34.

Bruce Winter argues that Paul was taken to the Areopagus, also referred to as Mars Hill, because it was believed that he was a herald of a foreign deity or deities. This was neither a trial nor a meeting for those interested in new religions! It was an initial hearing and, in time, a judgement would be made by a group of people who had some authority in deciding on matters relating to religious life in the city as to whether Paul's God was really a deity and whether he was suitable for inclusion in the Athenian Pantheon. Winter (1996:83) writes:

> Their courteousness is also in keeping with the fact that the herald [in this case Paul] would normally be a person of status and financial standing. The introduction of a new cult involved the herald buying the site, constructing an altar for sacrifices, providing a substantial benefaction for

---

[8] The Septuagint is the Greek translation of the Old Testament, which was originally written in Hebrew.

at least an annual dinner to honour the gods, and possibly providing support for cultic officials.

Of course, Paul is not going to buy land to construct a temple. His God is the Lord of the Heavens and the Earth who does not live in temples made by human hands. (Acts 17:24) Indeed, he is not advocating a new deity but explaining the nature of one who the Athenians already worshipped—the unknown God. Paul quotes from two poets with whom his audience would have been familiar. First, 'For in whom we live and move and have our being.' (Acts 17:28a) This is a quotation from Epimenides from Crete who we have already come across. Second, 'We are his offspring.' (Acts 17:28b) This phrase is accredited to Aratus from Cilicia who lived some 300 years after Epimenides. Both of these poems speak of Zeus as the supreme being of Greek and especially Stoic philosophy.

Paul makes no attempt to compare Zeus with God. He does, however, recognise two aspects of God's relationship with us: God provides us with life and we are created by him. The worship of something other than God displaces God from his rightful place as creator. Indeed, it displaces humankind from its rightful place as God's rulers on earth with real responsibility for others and all of creation.

Paul knew that the idea of resurrection from the dead was a concept his hearers would object to, and yet he keeps it at the core of his message. He has his eye on the coming judgement and courageously makes the case that God will judge the world with justice through His appointee, Jesus Christ, whom He raised from the dead. Some of us are tempted to hold back on saying something that will raise objections, or cause others to look down on us. Paul is direct; he is passing through the city, does not expect to have this opportunity again, and so does not edit out the resurrection account. Presumably he would have mentioned the life and death of Jesus, and so it would have been impossible for him to leave the story there. A new age had dawned with the life, death and resurrection of Jesus Christ, and God has not punished the worship of other gods and unknown gods as up until this point, such worship was based on a lack of understanding. Paul's message is that now God expects, in this new era, people to turn away from these practices and acknowledge Him as the true God who may be known because He has chosen to reveal Himself.

At any rate, this is God's mission, not Paul's, and this is clear from the results. Luke points out that some of the hearers sneered, some suspended judgement, and a few believed, including Dionysius (a member of the Areopagus), one lady named Damaris, and possibly others.

In Athens, Paul dealt with a variety of cultures and world views. There were Jews and God-fearing Gentiles in the synagogue. In the marketplace he would have come across local superstition, primal religion, occult practice, home-spun practical wisdom, approaches to life based on established Stoic and Epicurean philosophy, and, if that were not enough, new religious and philosophical ideas. At the Areopagus, Paul uses his knowledge of Greek literature to share his faith. If Bruce Winter is correct, Paul demonstrates an understanding of the purpose of the interview by the administrative council of the Areopagus—the request to have a new god included in the Athenian pantheon. Yet Paul uses the situation to communicate his message appropriately. All of this challenges us to become familiar with the different world views and cultural contexts we find ourselves in, both formal and informal.

Jeremiah, religious images and the nations

On my visits to Buddhist temples where I am usually surrounded by Buddhist images, I feel a sense of sadness that people for whom I have a great deal of affection do not know God in the way he wishes to be known. C. Wright (2006:177) comments:

> On the one hand, it is true that God battles with idolatry because it diminishes the glory that is rightly God's own. God's jealousy for God's own self is a powerful dynamic throughout Scripture. But, on the other hand, God's battle against the gods of human hands (and all they represent) can be seen as a function of his loving benevolence toward us and indeed toward his whole creation. Divine jealousy is in fact an essential function of divine love. It is precisely because God wills our good that he hates the self-inflicted harm that our idolatry generates. God's conflict with the gods is ultimately for our own good as well as for God's glory.

But we must not simply apply this to non-Christian religions! God cares for Christians too much to allow us to remain caught up in selfish ways and He exposes our priorities, relationships and ambitions which replace Him as the first focus of our lives. This is an essential function of divine love.

I certainly understand that many Buddhists are not worshipping the Buddha, but expressing appreciation for his discovery of the Truth of all things, the *Dhamma*, and his teaching of the path which leads away from suffering. That said, the words of Jeremiah 16:19-20, spoken some 200 years before the time of the Buddha, reflect something of my feelings:

O Lord, my strength and my fortress, my refuge in
the time of distress, to you the nations will come
from the ends of the earth and say 'Our fathers
possessed nothing but false gods, worthless idols
that did them no good. Do men make their own
gods? Yes, but they are not gods.'[9]

Is there a tinge of sadness to Jeremiah's words? Although referred to as the weeping prophet he robustly condemned the idolatry of his fellow Jews—yet here he appears to speak regretfully of non-Jewish religious traditions which had been handed down from generation to generation, but which were unable to meet the deep needs of their followers. However, hope shines through that these people will recognise the emptiness of their inherited tradition and see the fullness of what God offers, and that they will come to the Lord.

Abraham's concern for the people of Sodom and Gomorrah

There appears to be some similarity between Jeremiah's concern for the nations who have inherited a tradition that cannot really help them, and Abraham's prayer for the wicked people of Sodom and Gomorrah. I am not trying to make any comparison between the behaviour of some Buddhists and that of the people of Sodom and the other cities of the region. I have chosen to reflect on this passage because it portrays Abraham functioning as a representative of those who held a very different belief system to his own.

---

[9] For a very thorough treatment on God's response to idols, see chapter 5 'The Living God Confronts Idolatry' of C. Wright (2006). *The Mission of God*. Nottingham: IVP.

Abraham asks God if he would destroy the people of Sodom if there were 10 righteous people living there (Genesis 18:16-33). Some have suggested that this passage may have been a technique to show readers that these towns located in the valley of the Salt Sea were full of unrighteous people—even to the extent that not even 10 righteous people could be found living there. Clearly this justifies God's destruction of the people of the region, apart from Abraham's nephew Lot and his two daughters. The following chapter (Genesis 19) gives an account of the men of Sodom's intention to sexually assault the visitors who, although they looked like men, were in reality angelic beings. Indeed the men of Sodom also threatened Lot, an immigrant in good standing in their town. This complete disregard for the Middle Eastern value of hospitality, and the intention to sexually violate the visitors, indicates that these men were evil. Ezekiel (16:49-50) flags up other evil aspects of the nature of the people living in Sodom: they were 'arrogant, overfed and unconcerned; they did not help the poor and needy. They were haughty and did detestable things before me [God].'

Another understanding of Abraham's conversation with God (Genesis 18:16-33), and the one I wish to put forward, is that Abraham was functioning as a priest and representing the people of Sodom. (Keller, 2001) Abraham finds himself alone with the Lord as the Lord's two companions, who are variously referred to as angels and men, journey to Sodom. Prior to the departure of the two men, God asks them 'Shall I hide from Abraham what I am about to do?' He then goes on to say that he intends to destroy Sodom and Gomorrah because of their wickedness. We read that Abraham approached the Lord (18:23), a technical term for approaching a judge sitting in session. It may well be that the Lord's words in verse 19 gave Abraham a sense of God's purpose for him and his descendants, and that inspired him to converse with God, something he does with appropriate respect.

Abraham stands before the judge of the whole earth and asks that, if 50 righteous people were to be found in Sodom, the town might be spared. In a daring conversation with God, who has projected himself in human form into this situation, Abraham seems to be trying to work out whether, if a minimum number of righteous people were present in Sodom and Gomorrah, God would spare the city for their sake. The number of the required righteous people to be present to save these ungodly communities is lowered from 50 to 45, to 40, to 30, to 20 and finally to 10. The Lord answers that if there were 10 righteous people present, then the communities would not be destroyed. Why does Abraham stop asking at 10? I think he did very well to get to that point; carrying out this repeated questioning of the Lord was probably not a comfortable conversation to have. It may be that Abraham felt that the Lord had indicated his 'last price' was 10. Or, perhaps Abraham realised that there were not 10 righteous people in these places and that the Lord must bring about justice. This passage is the first account of intercessory prayer in Scripture. Here, we see Abraham with a concern not just for his nephew Lot and his family but also for the people who they lived among and who Abraham had previously helped. (see Genesis 14:12-16) Calvin (1992:486) supports this interpretation of the story when he comments 'I certainly do not doubt that he [Abraham] was so touched with a common compassion towards the five cities that he drew near as their intercessor.'

Justice is done, and the violent and selfish behaviour exhibited by both the young and the old men of Sodom towards Lot and his extra-terrestrial visitors surely confirm the 'rightness' of God's determination to do what He indicated to Abraham, to destroy Sodom and Gomorrah. God had heard the outcry against Sodom and Gomorrah and the outrageous sins that they had committed. People in the region would have cried out as a result of the cruel treatment that they suffered from the more powerful men from Sodom and Gomorrah. In a sense, the cry of the sufferer is a prayer for a just and powerful God to act on their behalf. Could the oppressed people of the villages of the plains have cried out in desperation to God, a God whom they did not know? Clearly we cannot say. Yet their wish for deliverance and justice was granted as the God of justice intervened on their behalf.

So what was the point of Abraham's intercession? C. Wright (2006:362) reminds us that Abraham's prayer had a good outcome in that the first request—'Will you sweep away the righteous with the wicked?' (Genesis 18:23)—was granted, as Lot and his two daughters were saved from destruction by escaping to Zoar. Wright goes on comment:

> Abraham is learning even as he is interceding. The God he is dealing with, the God who has taken him into his confidence for this very purpose, is prepared to be far more merciful than Abraham probably first hoped for.

The fashion-conscious females in my family often remind me that posture is everything! Our posture or attitude towards others and their beliefs is certainly important, and one of the key principles of working with people is that we will not be in their hearts until they see how much they are in our hearts. Abraham wondered if God may spare the unrighteous because of the righteous who were present. We now know that Christ, the righteous one will save the unrighteous many. Yet God involved Abraham in both prayer for the unrighteous and theological enquiry as to how He would deal with a mixed economy of righteous and unrighteous people. Jeremiah wept for his own people and looked forward to the time when all those who did not worship the Lord would leave their images, as well as the powers associated with them, who could not help. These two Old Testament examples—and there are others—call us to participate in God's work of reconciling the world to himself through Christ. Just as God drew near to Abraham and told him what he was going to do, so God calls us to be involved in his mission. (Compare this with Paul's words in 2 Corinthians 5:17-19.)

This account from the life of Abraham suggests that God wishes to enter into a genuine partnership with us. One aspect of partnership is that one will act differently from how one would have behaved if there was no partnership. There is an interaction between two minds; both minds are altered, and adaptation, accommodation and modification take place. Think of a father who is working in his garden. His young children want to help and he involves them. Left to himself the father would work in the garden in a particular way. 'Love does not insist on its own way' (1 Corinthians 13:5) and so the father adapts his plans and harnesses the good desires, creativity, and efforts of his children into the shaping of that part of his garden. It is not as the father had planned. The neighbours might not be impressed with the garden: the borders are not straight, and there is soil scattered on the grass, but the father enjoyed having his children work with him!

Karl Barth (1964:16) commented if we pray God will act in a different way than if we had not prayed. Intercessory prayer is when we pray on behalf of others and invite God into their situation. Sometimes our experience is that God does not seem to answer. This may partly be due to His respecting of the boundaries of others. Maybe God has to make people open to receive Him, or open to receive His help and that takes time. But surely, as a result of our prayers, God brings new possibilities into the lives of those we pray for.

I remember teaching one afternoon when I received a phone call from my wife saying that a Thai Buddhist friend who we had been praying for had just decided to become a follower of Jesus. Recently, I heard of a couple whom I know—the wife was a Buddhist and the husband a lapsed Christian—who have come to faith in Christ. When I heard of their conversion I was incredulous as I could not think of less likely candidates for faith in Christ. The Father is at work in the garden and He invites us to work with Him! From time to time we see the results of what He is doing and that encourages us to continue with a sense of purpose.

Pause for reflection

1. Paul has the capacity to switch between different Gospel presentations so that he may be best understood by the various types of people he engages with. He demonstrates awareness of different ideas and a mental nimbleness in switching quickly between approaches.

    What types of people do you engage with? How might you communicate more effectively with the group you find it hardest to speak to?

2. In Acts 17:22 to 34 we have a summary of Paul's talk at the Areopagus. What truths about God did Paul mention? You will find it helpful to check your findings with a commentary, such John Stott's commentary on Acts (*The Message of Acts*) pages 284 onwards.

Chapter 4

God and *Dhamma*: A starting point for the conversation?

In an interesting chapter in *Communicating Christ in Asian Cities*, the writer[1], a missionary in Thailand, sees similarity between the Greek word *logos* and the Buddhist term *Dhamma*. Indeed, he suggests that *Dhamma*, or *phratham* in Thai, might be a better translation for the Greek term *logos* used in John 1:1 and 14 than the 1984 Thai version which uses *phrawata*, 'word from the throne'.

This chapter examines the idea of using the Buddhist term *Dhamma* for God to give a Buddhist an initial understanding

---

[1] D. Von Stroh (2009). "Buddhadasa, Tamma, Jesus, and the Promise of New Creation". In: *Communicating Christ in Asian Cities*. Ed. by P. De Neui. Pasadena, California: William Carey Library, pp. 225–259.

of whom Christians consider to be the Ultimate or Absolute. As we read this chapter, Christians may develop an appreciation for the difficulty that a Buddhist has with the Christian insistence that that which is Absolute, the God of the Christian understanding, is also personal and relational.

Some Buddhist understandings of the *Dhamma*

When written with a lower case *d*, *dhamma* refers to the building blocks of all that exists. These are interdependent basic patterns which exist and contribute to the apparent substantial or permanent appearance of something or someone. In this sense, *dhamma* is similar to 'quarks' in physics. These *dhamma*s will be viewed as either 'real' or 'empty of reality' depending on one's understanding of the nature of reality. For example, Madhyamaka philosophy would say that what 'we experience does not exist in an absolute sense, but only in a relative way, as a passing phenomenon.'

Dhamma, with the upper case *D*, is not just a Buddhist term; it is an Indian concept, with a variety of philosophical and social understandings. The term derives from a Sanskrit root which means 'to maintain' or 'to hold'; if you follow the *Dhamma*, it will hold you back from suffering. In Vedic literature, *Dhamma* was a term used to denote the sacrifices made to maintain the 'order of the cosmos'. (Buswell and Lopez, 2013:242) *Dhamma* simply is; it is not dependent on anything or anyone. Yet it is not just the way things are; it is also the way we should act 'if we are to avoid bringing harm to both ourselves and others'. (Gethin, 1998) In other words, it is the practice of that which is true, and in that sense it should be seen as a skill as well as a body of knowledge.

Some Buddhist understandings of the *Dhamma*

The *Dhamma* is one of the three aspects of the Triple Gem. Used in this sense, it refers to the Buddha's path and its goal of *nibbāna*. (Harvey, 1995:3) The other two gems are the Buddha and the *saṅgha*, the community of Buddhists; in some traditions, this is understood as being made up solely of the monks. A Buddhist seeks refuge in these three aspects of the tradition, and venerates the Buddha as the one who discovered the *Dhamma*. Because of many generations of moral failure, the *Dhamma* was no longer understood by humanity. Not only did the Buddha discover the *Dhamma*, the truths which underpin everything, he discovered it by himself as he had no teacher. In that sense, a Buddha's wisdom and achievement is so much greater than that of other enlightened beings who have had the benefit of instruction. After discovering the *Dhamma* by himself, the Buddha did not remain an enlightened recluse, a solitary Buddha[2], but became a skilful travelling teacher who taught the *Dhamma* and formed the *saṅgha*. At the heart of the *saṅgha* is the monastic community who model the teachings of the Buddha and teach the *Dhamma* to lay Buddhists, as well as giving pastoral care and instruction in the practice of the *Dhamma*, such as meditation.

After coming to understand the truth of all things the Buddha commented:

> This *Dhamma* that I have found is profound, hard to see, hard to understand; it is peaceful, sublime, beyond the sphere of mere reasoning, subtle, to be experienced by the wise. But this generation takes delight in attachment, is delighted by attachment, rejoices in attachment and as such it is hard for them to see this truth, namely *nirvāṇa*. (*Majjhima Nikāya* 1:167)

---

[2] Sanskrit '*pratyeka*-Buddha.'

The Buddhist tradition recounts how the great god, the Brahmā Sahampati, stood before the Buddha and asked him to teach the *Dhamma*, saying that there were those who had but little dust in their eyes and would be able to easily grasp it. (*Majjhima Nikāya* 1:167) This led to the newly enlightened Buddha going to the five ascetics he had practised with and preaching his first sermon.[3] The Buddha's role of teacher and modeller of the *Dhamma*, as well as the instigator of the *saṅgha*, has an echo in Christianity. Christ reveals the truths about God and how He wishes people to live, through words, through deeds, what he says and how he lives. Like the Buddha, he called his disciples to be with him and to hear his life-changing teaching. It was out of Jesus Christ's '*saṅgha*' that the Church emerged—counter-cultural communities that pointed to what life will one day be like under God's rule.

The Buddha, however, made the point that the *Dhamma* is not an end in itself; its function is to point to enlightenment. In 'The Parable of the Raft', the Buddha compares the *Dhamma* to a raft which a person constructs when he needs to cross a wide stretch of water. When the person crosses over the

---

[3] This is referred to as the first turning of the wheel of the *Dhamma*, or *Dhamma Cakka Pavattana Sutta*. According to Buddhists in the Mahāyāna and Vajrayāna (Tibetan) traditions there are two further turnings of the *Dhamma* wheel.

The second turning of the wheel of the *Dhamma* refers to the concept of emptiness, *suññatā*, and its implications. If there is nothing of substance to a thing—for instance, a car, or even a good reputation—then why strive after and hold on to these things? This idea of the emptiness of things is an extension of the Buddha's teaching on *anatta*, the emptiness, or lack of a substantial fixed essence, of self. This emerged with the Madhyamaka school; a key thinker in this fraternity was Nāgārjuna, the South Indian philosopher monk who lived around CE 150 to 250.

The third turning of the wheel of the *Dhamma* occurred around 200 years later and refers to the Yogācāra tradition which viewed the true nature of everything as a construction of the mind. Indeed, the Zen tradition draws on Yogācāra ideas, such as the use of the *Lankāvatāra Sūtra* which was translated into Chinese around 420 CE.

water, they do not carry the raft over the land, even though the raft had been useful to them. Anything which helps us gain enlightenment may be viewed as *Dhamma*, but it is to be understood as a means to an end, rather than the end. The 'Parable of the Raft' ends with the Buddha saying 'The *Dhamma* taught by me [is] for crossing over, not retaining.' (*Majjhima-Nikāya* 1:134, translated by Horner, 1954) The *Dhamma* is the truth of all things, and the laws which underpin our universe. Many Buddhists, however, say that it is unwise to be over-reliant on the *Dhamma*, or use it to support ideas that it was never designed to undergird.

The *Dhammakāya*, the body of the *Dhamma*, is normally understood by Theravādin Buddhists as being the teachings and moral greatness of the Buddha, and which today is compiled in the Pali canon. It is the absolute truth of all things. Mahāyāna Buddhism, on the other hand, understands *Dhammakāya* as the buddha-nature which resides within all sentient beings. *Dhammakāya* contains ultimate truth and all the qualities necessary to be a Buddha, and it is realised at enlightenment.

'This *Dhamma* that I have found is profound, hard to see, hard to understand; it is peaceful, sublime, beyond the sphere of mere reasoning, subtle, to be experienced by the wise'. I would like to use this quotation from the Buddha in the *Majjhima Nikāya* to inform our understanding of the *Dhamma*. The Buddha speaks here of the *Dhamma* as mysterious, beautiful, yet capable of being experienced by the wise. Perhaps Grimm (1994:301) is right when he translates the *Dhamma* which the Buddha discovered as 'the Marvel.' (*ayam dhammo*). We noted earlier that *dhamma* with a lower case *d* was a term used for a 'thing', and Grimm is at pains to point out that this 'thing' can also be interpreted as a 'thing in itself', or the 'best thing', *saddhamma*, which he translates as 'Marvel'.

I wonder if there are some commonalities between this particular understanding of *Dhamma* and God. Of course, any identified similarities may only be tentative and suggestive. It is my hope that any emerging ideas could be used to create a space for those from a non-theistic religion to stop and reflect on the One who Christians say is mysterious, beautiful and yet capable of being experienced.

Venerable Buddhadasa's understanding of the *Dhamma*

The missionary mentioned at the beginning of this chapter wrote that his Thai Buddhist friend was comfortable with using *'Prajaow'* ('God') and *'Dhamma'* interchangeably, but laughed at the concept of God being a person. The missionary's Buddhist friend explained:

> God cannot be a person because God is infinite and eternal, there is no beginning and no end to God, he does not have a day he was born and a day he will die and be no more, he is all powerful and all knowing.

Apparently, the friend of the missionary had been a Buddhist monk for 10 years and was familiar with the writings of the Venerable Buddhadasa Indeppano, the well known Thai scholar monk.[4] It would seem appropriate, then, to now engage with Buddhadasa and his efforts at encouraging Buddhist - Christian understanding vis-à-vis the *Dhamma*.

---

[4] Buddhadasa (1906-1993) was born in South Thailand, then called Siam. He was ordained as a monk in 1926. After study in Bangkok, he returned home in 1932, the year the country changed from being an absolute to a constitutional monarchy. Buddhadasa began to live in an abandoned temple which was renamed Suan Mokkhaphalaram. He moved to a new location some 11 years later but the new temple is still called Suan Mokkh, the 'Garden

Back in 1969, in a lecture entitled *Dhamma-The World Saviour*, Buddhadasa said: 'If we substitute the word *Dhamma* for God, then there can be no misunderstanding, for God is truth, truth is God, and always so, because it means an impersonal god, which is *Dhamma*.' In a short book entitled *Reply to a Catholic Father*, Buddhadasa noted that in Buddhism there is no clear reference to God and commented:

> "God" is only the natural law which governs the universe and if Christians would interpret the word "God" as natural law, Buddhism and Christianity could be at one. But if Christians insist on seeing God as a person, the two cannot be in accord, for Buddhism has no personal God and no reference to God as a person.

Buddhadasa understood the Christian explanation of God as 'personal' to be simple and immature. It was an 'everyday understanding' which needed to mature into a deeper

---

of Liberation'. Currently there are around 40 monks living at the temple, a figure which increases to around 70 during the yearly 'rains retreat' (*phansa*). Additionally, over 1000 Westerners visit Suan Mokkhaphalaram each year.

Buddhadasa wrote a number of significant books and creatively engaged with Christianity as well as drawing a number of terms and ideas from Zen Buddhism. He had a view that society should be based on and governed by the *Dhamma*. Such a society would be characterised by: the good of the whole, restraint and generosity, and respect and loving kindness. (D.K Swearer, 2005:1073) Buddhadasa's re-interpretation of ideas such as rebirth and *nibbāna*, as well as his pro-rational, anti-superstitious approach made Buddhism much more accessible and relevant to a well educated, middle class audience. There is a real sense that he lives on in his teaching. It is as he wrote:

> Even when I die and the body ceases,
> My voice still echoes in comrade's ears,
> Clear and bright, as loud as ever,
> Just as I never died, the *Dhamma*-body lives on. (D.K Swearer, 2005:1073)

awareness which acknowledged that the 'father figure' was something of a projection of the Christian's need for security. Elsewhere Buddhadasa writes:

> God in general understanding is god in terms of *phasakhon* [every day language or conventional understanding] which has not been developed to a higher understanding of God as in *phasatham* ['*Dhamma* language' or 'ultimate understanding']... For ease and practicality in the discussion, god in terms of *phasakhon* is god that is described as having shape or form, able to love, or be angered, who requires this and that, can do right and wrong etc. whereas god in *phasatham* has no shape or form, remains constant and unchangeable, therefore does not love, is not angry, is beyond having any needs, beyond doing right and wrong. (Quoted in Boon-Itt, 2007:118)

Buddhadasa is well known for his *phasakhon/phasatham* hermeneutic —the distinction between everyday language and *Dhamma* language. He writes:

> Everyday language is worldly language, the language of people who do not know *Dhamma*. *Dhamma* language is spoken by people who have gained a deep insight into the truth, *Dhamma*. Having perceived *Dhamma*, they speak in terms appropriate to their experience, and so *Dhamma* language comes to be. (D.K. Swearer, 1989:126)

Thus, an element of enlightenment is required before a person may understand what the teachings of the Buddha mean.

This raises a number of interesting issues. Let me just mention one in passing. The Apostle Paul writes 'The man without the Spirit does not accept the things that come from the Spirit of God, for they are foolishness to him, and he cannot understand them, because they are spiritually discerned.' (1 Corinthians 2:14) Paul's idea here of dependence on God to understand the Christian Scriptures may not resonate with a Buddhist, because in Buddhism, one must prove the truth of the teaching one has received.

For Buddhadasa, some level of enlightenment is required to interpret the teachings of the Buddha. Presumably, if enlightenment is insight into truth then enlightenment gained in the Buddhist tradition gives one the ability to interpret the teaching and texts of any religious tradition. For the Buddhist, reliance on someone else—especially God, a figure not found in Buddhism—is an inadequate basis for interpreting! Christians take the view that openness to God to make the Christian Scriptures clear is an essential feature of a good interpretative process. This 'openness' does not bypass careful scholarship; rather, it is an engaging with the divine intelligence which influenced the writing of the Christian Scriptures.

Varasak (1996:303), who studied under Buddhadasa, recommends that Buddhists who are asked if there is a God in Buddhism should ask for a definition of God. If the response is that God is the Supreme *Being*, then Varadhammo advises the Buddhist to say that yes, we have a God in Buddhism, but our God is the supreme *Thing*, which is *Dhamma,* the Law of Nature. 'The Law of Nature is the God in Buddhism, a non-personal God'.

Some Buddhists may accept the concept of Ultimate Truth or Reality, the *Dhamma*, as an impersonal God. Others, however, will not take that view. British born Sangharakshita, who founded the Friends of the Western Buddhist Order[5] in 1967, comments on how it is in the nature of the *Dhamma* to dispel false views. Clearly Sangharakshita (1987:470) has in mind the Christian tradition when he writes:

> The Bodhisattva can no longer preach the *Dhamma* without refuting such wrong views as a belief in a creator God and an unchanging individual self than it is possible for the sun to rise without dispelling the darkness.

Jesus as *Dhamma*?

The word 'Word' in John 1:1 and 14 refers to God in human form: Jesus Christ. The writer of John's Gospel understands 'Word', or *Logos* in the Greek in which the Scripture was originally written, as the first cause of all created things and beings. In addition, he uses the term to indicate that God came in human form in order to engage with humankind. These two verses are multi-faceted and have many important themes such as that Word, Jesus Christ, coming in human form and perfectly keeping God's laws, first as a craftsman in a village in Palestine and then as a homeless teacher travelling with his disciples.

In the first five books of the Christian Scriptures—the Hebrew *Torah*, also known in Greek as the *Pentateuch*—we encounter the concepts of law and truth which circumscribe the Jewish tradition; the Ten Commandments, for example, point to the nature of God, the importance of community, and the way that we should live. The Christian belief is that Jesus Christ

---

[5] Now known as Triratna.

not only fulfilled the Jewish *Torah*, but that he also revealed God and the way to God. In the *Saṃyutta Nikāya* 22:87, the Buddha comforts the sick monk Vakkali who wanted to see the Buddha before he died. The Buddha said 'Enough, Vakkali. Why do you want to see this filthy body? Whoever sees the *Dhamma* sees me: whoever sees me sees the *Dhamma*.' Buddhists draw a close connection between *Dhamma* and their teacher—after all, the Buddha discovered the *Dhamma*. Christians see Jesus Christ as embodying truth and living out a perfect life. Indeed, in a response to a statement by Philip, one of his disciples, Christ says 'Anyone who has seen me has seen the Father.' (John 14:9)

Earlier in the same passage, Jesus Christ indicates that he *is* the truth. Could we say that Christ is *Dhamma*? In the life and teachings of Christ, truth is demonstrated to humanity. Christ also goes on to say that he is the way to the end of the journey. This is a response to a perplexed disciple, speaking on behalf of the others, who knew neither the destination, nor the way. Christ indicates that he is on a journey back to where he came from—the Father. Like the Buddha, Christ does not overly discuss the destination but does disclose the path. In the Buddhist tradition, an enlightened being experiences *nibbāna* in the 'here and now' prior to passing over to the far shore where he will enter a new, dimensionless existence. In a similar way, one who follows Jesus Christ reaps the benefits of that relationship, and believes that it points to a state of even greater well-being after this life on earth, a state of eternal life.

If God is the equivalent of the *Dhamma*, and if Jesus Christ is God come in the flesh, then clearly Jesus is also the equivalent of the *Dhamma*. The formless takes on form and the *Dhamma* is modelled through the speech and actions of Jesus, the Son of God. Just as one's character is expressed through physical actions, so Jesus Christ expresses the invisible, divine nature. In earlier times, as the Jewish people travelled through the desert from Egypt to Israel, God had signified his presence by a cloud during the day and a pillar of fire by night. After that, the tabernacle was located among the Jews, whether they were in their tents or travelling. This portable sanctuary symbolised God's glorious presence and was eventually replaced by a temple twice the size of the tabernacle. This intricate building involved the labour of many thousands of craftsmen over a seven year period and was completed in 959 BCE under King Solomon's leadership, only to be destroyed by the Babylonians around 586 BCE.

A second temple, a much more modest building, was completed in 516 BCE, around 35 years before the birth of the one who would become the Buddha. This was destroyed by the Romans in 70 CE, after a four year siege of the city of Jerusalem. The writer of John's Gospel sees the 'Word' as meaning God come in human form, not just present simply as a religious symbol. In the past, God's presence filled the tabernacle and later it filled the temple as a radiant glory, signifying that God was present with his people. Now that glory is seen in God in human form: Jesus Christ.

Of course, not everyone recognised this glory. In particular, the religious elite were blinded by their anger at Jesus' challenge to their religious practice. Because Jesus appeared in a culture which was expecting the coming of a Messiah who would be a divinely-appointed liberator, he was *not* recognised as being that person. If he had an agenda to liberate the Jewish people from the Romans, he surely would have been accepted as the Messiah. Not only was he not recognised as being God, or even as being from God, but he was rejected by the vast majority of his people. Ultimately, this rejection resulted in his execution.

There were, however, a few who recognised the special nature of God come in human form. For such, Jesus Christ is viewed as the 'One and Only, who came from the Father'. Speaking of his (and the other disciples') experience of God who had come as a human, the writer of John's Gospel reflects:

> The Word became flesh and made his dwelling among us. The Word (*Logos*) [put in the word *Dhamma* to see if it fits] became flesh and made his dwelling among us. We have seen his glory, the glory of the One and Only, who came from the Father, full of grace and truth. (John 1:14)

There is the idea here of God becoming human and pitching his tent among the other campers and being subject to the benefits and disadvantages of camping just like everyone else! Rienecker and Rogers (1980:219) comment that 'the flesh of Jesus Christ is the new localization of God's presence on earth.' Christ replaces the tabernacle (tent) and the temple where the glory of God[6] appeared. John and the other disciples observed Christ in difficult situations. They saw him as he taught, healed, helped and reacted under various kinds of intense pressure. In all of this the observers note the glory of God in human form and mention in particular this glory being characterised by 'grace and truth'. In this text which we have referred to (John 1:14) the reliability and dependability of Jesus Christ is flagged up by reference to 'truth', while 'grace' signifies the loving kindness (*mettā*) Christ shows to those who follow him—a gift and not a reward!

Buddhists such as Cabezón (2000:26), an Indo-Tibetan Buddhist scholar, may well understand God come in human form as a *nirmāṇakāya*, the projection of an enlightened being into our world in order to show people the path to liberation from

---

[6] In Hebrew, the *shekinah*.

suffering. Such a projection would not deny that the being associated with it is enlightened; it, however, merely questions the corporeality of the appearance. This was an issue in the early church as the docetic movement understood falsely that the humanity of Jesus Christ was an illusory appearance. The term comes from the Greek *dokien* meaning 'to appear', or 'to seem'. A typical docetic view of Jesus Christ was he was revealed as a man, but this was not a 'real body'. Referring a Buddhist friend to the *Definition of Calcedon* (451 CE) where Jesus Christ is described as being truly God and truly man is, I suppose, a possibility—but words which cannot be proved are not readily entertained by Buddhists! Experience, however, may be part of proof and God come in human form invites people to experience him, not simply understand words about him. The result of such openness may be an encounter out of which a trustful confidence or faith (Pali *saddhā*) emerges or, indeed, in which the free gift of faith is received.

German theologian Deitrich Bonhoeffer (1959:53), who was executed by the Nazis at the end of the World War II in 1945, writes that 'the road to faith passes through obedience to the call of Jesus'. If you believe, then take the first step; if you don't believe, *still* take the first step—it may lead to faith! For some, faith only comes from stepping out into the unknown; it is only then that the path is discovered. In discussing Jesus' call to people to follow him Bonhoeffer uses an enigmatic couplet reminiscent of a Zen *koān*—only he who believes is obedient, and only he who is obedient believes.

What exactly do we mean when we say God is 'personal'?

From a Buddhist perspective, personal existence implies being subject to change and dependence on something else; in this case, whatever else, God cannot be personal. Christians insist that God knows us and that we might know him; he is personal, and wants us to enter into a relationship with him. Is there any way out of this impasse? Can we encourage our Buddhist friends to consider a different perspective? In *Christianity and the World Religions*, Hans Küng (1993:393-4) uses an approach used in Buddhism to challenge a rigid understanding of particular views—something that is considered to be unhelpful practice by Buddhists. Let me sum up Küng's four-cornered negation approach.

First, Küng denies that the Absolute is personal. God is *not* some sort of superman. If he were, then 'the all-encompassing and all penetrating One would become an object, which man would have "at his disposal" which he could put into words'. (Küng, 1993:394) The Absolute is not an individual among others and, while there is a place for speaking about God as if he were human (anthropomorphic language), we need to take care that comparisons do not create misunderstandings.

Second, Küng denies that the Absolute is impersonal. The laws of the cosmos which have been proved and those yet to be discovered, along with the fundamental forces of the universe, were brought into being by the Absolute. They are, however, distinct from him. That being the case, it is not appropriate to refer to God as a force, or set of laws.

Third, Küng denies that the Absolute is *both* personal *and* impersonal. He finds it hard to imagine anything meaningful coming from such a combination. Is Keith Ward (1984:4) disagreeing with Küng when he comments: 'Nothing in the universe can ever be separated from God, and so everything is "in him"; yet all finite things have their own proper being which makes them quite distinct'? Ward encourages us to think of God as an unlimited reality of which all things, from us as individuals to the galaxies, are part. Certainly, the Christian Scriptures present Jesus Christ as the creator of all things in heaven and earth whether they be visible or invisible and 'in him all things hold together'. (Colossians 1:15-20) I think Ward's view is non-Newtonian rather than an argument for pantheism, the idea that there is no distinction between God and creation. God is present *to* but distinct *from* all of his creation, a view sometimes referred to as panentheism.

Fourth, Küng denies that the Absolute is *neither* personal *nor* impersonal. That would be nihilistic and Christians believe that there is substance or 'fullness' to the nature of God. God is full of what makes him God. Indeed, not only is there substance (fullness) to the Absolute, Ephesians 1:23 views God as filling everything in every way. Saint Paul prays to God for new believers who had recently come out of an occult background (Ephesians 3:19) to have the power or capacity to understand the boundless *mettā* or love of Christ, despite it being beyond human knowledge. The purpose of these people being 'filled to the measure of all the fullness of God' is for them to enter, in practical terms, into their new identity. It is not that they need to love Christ more, rather that they need to know how much they are loved by Christ. Effort was required in following this new way, for to be a Christian in the first century CE was to be viewed by both strict Jews and Romans alike as being subversive. There was the sheer audacity of living as a first century follower of Jesus as *the* Lord and bringer of peace, through being crucified on a Roman cross. This was dangerous counter-cultural living in an empire which confessed Caesar as Lord and where peace (the *Pax Romana*) was enforced by military domination. Following Jesus Christ in the Middle East at the beginning of the 21st century is still hugely challenging.

The fullness of the Absolute may then be viewed as a boundless energy which benevolently operates according to all aspects of the nature of God as described in the Christian Scriptures. These include: purity, compassion and justice. At the macro level, this boundless intelligent energy upholds the cosmos: at a micro level, it wishes to engage positively with individuals and communities. A key concept in Buddhism is emptiness (*suññatā*). Emptiness does not mean that there is nothing there, but out-with *nibbāna* no person or substance has a firm or fixed nature. A secondary but important meaning of *suññatā* is the interconnected nature and openness of all things to everything for good or ill. I look at the tree which almost touches my office window and see the trunk, branches and leaves. I may think that there is nothing in the tree that does not belong to the tree but the tree has made connections with water, air, earth and sunlight. The existence of this healthy tree demonstrates an openness and connection to these key elements. Dogen, the 13th century Japanese Zen master, remarked 'When the old plum tree is in bloom then the whole world is in its blossom.' Buddhists have challenged me to meditate and let go of my theistic attachments in order to experience reality. But might Buddhists let go of their conviction that there is no God to see if a faith in God arises within them? After all, Saint Paul in his talk at the *Aerogapus* in Athens said God created us in such a way that we 'would seek him and find him, though he is not far from each one of us. For in him [God] we live and move and have our being.' (Acts 17:27-28) Karl Reichelt, whom we read about in chapter one comments:

> 'Faith' is, therefore, something much more than 'blind belief'. Faith means that a new faculty is set free in my life, a faculty with the most tremendous working radius, a faculty which brings me, an earth bound, feeble and limited being, into con-

tact with the Divine, the Eternal, the Boundless.
Eilert (Quoted in 1974:111)

God is so much greater than we can conceive of when we use the term 'personal'. Küng suggests that while speaking of God 'transpersonal' may be a better term than 'personal'. This may be helpful if 'transpersonal' is understood to mean that which lies beyond all that we humans understand by the term 'personal'. The term 'transpersonal' may create a sense of mystery—a way of being that is beyond human understanding, and this may prove helpful to Buddhists. The term, however, should not be used to negate the relational attributes of God's nature. The Buddha explained that a 'person's' existence in *nibbāna* was beyond our understanding, yet that should not prevent our journey towards this state of bliss. Buddhists, then, may pursue the path to an enlightenment which they do not yet understand, but which they believe is both real and worth reaching. For the God-seeker, God is both the one that is being sought and the one who makes it possible for Him to be found.

God is unconditioned, yet causes everything else to be dependent on Him. We may say that He has a boundlessness in terms of space, an eternity in terms of time, and a perfection in terms of morality. God is unique in the sense that He may not be divided into parts. And so, when we speak of the unoriginated divine community of Father, Son and Holy Spirit, we are not thinking of three separate units of the Godhead. All of the Godhead is in the Father and the Eternal Son and the Holy Spirit, and each person of the Trinity is always in the other two; the theological term for this is *perichoresis*. These three persons are one God, identical in substance, and equal in power and glory. They have, however, specific and differing functions, as American theologian Stanley Grenz (2000:67) explains:

> The Father functions as the ground of the world and of the divine programme for creation. The Son functions as the revealer of God, the exemplar and herald of the Father's will for creation, and the redeemer of humankind. And the Spirit functions as the personal divine power active in the world, the completer of the divine will and programme.

Each person in the Trinity is dedicated to the others not only in the restoring of all things to their original purpose, but also in an eternal and uniting love (*mettā*). Jesus talks about this Trinitarian love in his prayer to the Father; that he will continue, through the Holy Spirit, to make the Father known 'in order that the love you [the Father] have for me [the Son] might be in them [the disciples]'. (John 17:26) Of course, the Son speaking to the Father is an example of the relational aspect and personality that we have been talking about.

Certainly the different roles but common aim of the Godhead is not lost on Buddhadasa (1967:109) who comments:

> The Father in Heaven may be thought of as the owner of an enormously vast quarry of gems. The Son—Jesus Christ—is the man who brings forth the gems for distribution to all mankind. The Spirit (or the Soul) represents those gems. These three are one. They all have gems in common. Their functions are in union and inseparable.

Buddhadasa goes on to compare the Christian trinity to the Triple Gem (the Buddha, the monastic community and the teachings of Buddha). He suggests that the Buddha discovers an immense store of gems, the *Dhamma*. The monastic community takes these gems into the world. How do you as a Christian working in a Buddhist context respond to or build on Buddhadasa's ideas?

Should we compare God to the *Dhamma* or the Buddha?

In discussing the Triple Gem, Jose Ignacio Cabezón (2000:22) comments that it is the *Dharma* which constitutes the core of the Buddhist tradition. He observes:

> The doctor (Buddha) may diagnose the problem and prescribe the cure, the nursing staff (*saṅgha*) may administer it and help the paitent in the process of recovery, but it is the medicine (*Dharma*, as embodied in the Buddha's teaching and internalized in the lives of his followers) that is the real antidote to the illness.

This may support the argument for juxtaposing the term *Dhamma* with God. On the other hand, the abbot of the Thai Buddhist temple in Edinburgh recently said to me that the Buddha was greater than the *Dhamma*, as he discovered it by himself. From a Buddhist perspective, the vital principles which underpin existence and hold the key for our liberation from suffering were both discovered and experienced by the Buddha. Buddhists maintain that they were then explained with a clarity which resulted quickly in the enlightenment of many. An obvious example would be the Buddha's first sermon where the five world-renouncers he had practised with understood his exposition of the Four Noble Truths and acknowledged that he had discovered the *Dhamma*.

The abbot felt that the best Buddhist term to use for God or Christ would be 'Buddha'. When discussing faith in the two traditions, Sangharakshita (1987:312) comments 'For God we have to substitute the Buddha, not because of any similarity in their nature and functions, but because of the equipollency of their respective positions.' Of course, one of the conditions for being a Buddha is to be born into the life in which enlightenment takes place—in Jambudvipa, the general region of India, into a priestly or noble family. If we hold tightly to this, we cannot make Jesus into a Buddha! Perhaps the real issue is to *which* Buddha might we compare Christ. Gotama, the historical Buddha, is neither the first, nor the last Buddha. Indeed, in the *Buddhavamsa* (Lineage of the Buddhas) in the *Khuddaka-Nikāya*, the lives of 27 Buddhas prior to Gautama are mentioned, and a further 13 Buddhas after Maitreya, the next Buddha. Could the Amitāba Buddha be compared to Christ? This would offer the opportunity to compare Christianity with Pure Land Buddhism, which has the concept of salvation through depending on the merit and kindness of Amitāba.

When we think of the term 'Buddha', we need to think beyond the physical being of Gotama, the historical Buddha. The *Tri-kaya* or triple-body doctrine, which emerged in the Mahāyāna school of Buddhism, posits three aspects of Buddhahood. There is the transformation body, *nirmāṇakāya*, where a Buddha appears in human form. This is understood to be physical projection of an enlightened being into another world in order to deliver the inhabitants—in our case, humankind—from suffering. They are simply teaching devices. Indeed, Harvey (1990:126) mentions that D.T. Suzuki viewed some religious teachers from non-Buddhist traditions as transformation-bodies, appearing in a form appropriate to a particular culture.

The second body is referred to as the enjoyment body, *sambhogakāya*. This body is adopted by heavenly Buddhas for their own enjoyment, as well as the benefit and development of Bodhisattvas who have the capacity to discern this subtle body.

The third body is known as the *Dhamma* body, *Dhammakāya*. It is seen by some traditions, particularly within Theravāda Buddhism, as the teachings of the Buddha contained within the Buddhist Scriptures, and what we should focus on in terms of belief and practice. In the Wat Phra Dhammakāya tradition, which emerged from the teachings of Luang Phaw Sot (1885-1959) at Wat Paknam, Bangkok, *Dhammakāya* is not subject to impermanence, suffering and no-self: it is the Buddha-nature which exists within each person, and provides the potential for enlightenment. The Yogācāra school tend to view *Dhammakāya* as 'what is known and realised on attaining Buddhahood, it is *nirvāṇa*.' (Harvey, 1990:127) In the Zen tradition, one finds a well known enigmatic statement which says, 'If you meet the Buddha on the road; kill him!' The idea here is that we should be focusing not on the *nirmāṇakāya*, the human form of the Buddha, but rather on the *Dhammakāya* the teachings of the Buddha, or indeed the Buddha-nature within. Coomaraswamy (1916:239) compares *Dhammakāya* to God the Father, the *sambhogakāya* to Christ in glory, and the *nirmāṇakāya* to Jesus Christ, the Eternal Son come in the flesh.

If we were to compare God to a Buddha, perhaps a fruitful avenue would be to use the Ādi Buddha. This Buddha is referred to as self-originating, and was present before anything else existed. Keown (2003:5) remarks that both rebirth (*saṃsāra*) and enlightenment arise from the nature of the Ādi Buddha. It may be understood as the original Buddha nature from which all Buddhas emerge. There is some resonance here with the eternal, unoriginated nature of God. Some comparison may also be made between the Buddha-nature, which Buddhists believe exists in all sentient beings, and the image of God (*imago Dei*) which Christians believe is within each person. Just as the Buddha-nature may point to the original source of the primordial Buddha, so the *imago Dei* points to God. Buddhadasa (1967:105) anticipates this comparison and notes that from the

> Ādi Buddha comes the various historical Buddhas, such as Gotama Buddha, Jesus etc., each having appeared at a different time according to the circumstances. The concepts are undoubtedly parallel. If you agree that God is "Dhamma" then we can safely say that *Dhamma is the womb of everybody* including the prophets or the teachers.

The Ādi Buddha is a concept with which many within the Vajrayāna (Tibetan) tradition are familiar. Many within this tradition will associate the Primordial Buddha with Vairocana, normally the central figure in the *maṇḍala* of the five Buddhas.[7] McArthur (2004:35) comments:

> Vairocana is considered by many Buddhists, particularly in Japan, to be the Supreme Buddha or

---

[7] The *maṇḍala* is a sacred circle representing a sacred realm. It often consists of concentric circles, enclosed by a square, all contained within a sacred circular boundary. The *maṇḍala* contains 'symbols and images that depict aspects of the enlightened psycho-physical personality of the Buddha and that indicate Buddhist themes and concepts'. Powers, 1995:227

the Cosmic Buddha the embodiment of the Historical Buddha and his *Dharma*. In certain schools of Northern Buddhism, Vairocana also corresponds to the Ādi Buddha, a primordial, omniscient Buddha, who created the universe, and all other Buddhas.

If Vairocana is viewed as a representation of Ādi Buddha, then we have to think through several issues. First, who do the other four Buddhas represent?[8] Second, to what extent, for the purpose of communicating Christian truth, should we try to engage with the associated characteristics and qualities of Vairocana? For example, Vairocana is understood as having an illuminating function as teacher of the *Dhamma*, and possessing the quality of wisdom by which ignorance is overcome. His throne is a lion, his colour white and is associated with having White Tārā as a consort. A fairly literal approach may have merit in a Tibetan folk context. In my office, I have a print of a *thangka* painting in the Tibetan tradition, produced by a Nepalese painter, depicting 12 scenes from the life of Christ based on the Tibetan wheel of life.[9] It sympathetically follows the genre of the Tibetan style, without colonizing it. In a similar way, a sacred circle representing a sacred realm (*maṇḍala*) based on some of the vivid imagery or even depicting the cosmic encounter between the white and black forces

---

[8] The other four Buddhas of the *maṇḍala* are Amitabha in the west, Aksobhya in the east, Amoghasiddhi in the north and Ratnasambhava in the south. These Buddhas are referred to as Dhyani (meditation) Buddhas; it would be more accurate to refer to them as the five *tathagātas*.

[9] Tibetan paintings usually depict Buddhist deities and pure lands. The rich symbolism is helpful for teaching, or functioning as an object for meditation and/or devotion. Often there is use made of the *bhāvacakra* or 'wheel of life'. The painting of a *thangka* calls for skill and focus and is an act of meditation in itself. It is also viewed as being a meritorious activity.

contained in the Book of Revelation may help those in the Tibetan and some Mahāyāna traditions become familiar with Christian understandings of what the future holds, and who holds the future.

Conclusion

We began by asking if comparing God with the *Dhamma* was appropriate from an Evangelical Christian perspective. In saying that Christ is Truth, it may be argued that he models the *Dhamma*. We noted that the Venerable Buddhadasa advocated the idea that God is the equivalent of the *Dhamma* and took the view that Christians who understood God as 'personal' are misguided. Indeed, he suggested that they needed to move on from an everyday understanding to a more mature, deeper-level understanding. We looked at what we *mean* when we say that God is personal, and tried to follow Hans Küng's four cornered negation of the view that God is personal. Küng's conclusion was that 'transpersonal' may be a more suitable term than 'personal' to describe God. For Christians who wish to discuss their faith with Tibetan Buddhists then the expression of Christian ideas through *thangkas* and *maṇḍalas* may be worth exploring. Such Christians may also be interested in comparing God with the Primordial or Ādi Buddha, referred to sometimes as Vairocana; the central or supreme Buddha in the Five Buddha *maṇḍala*.

Comparing God to the *Dhamma* is a penultimate way of describing God to Buddhists. There still, however, lies the challenge of demonstrating that this ultimate intelligence is both relational and good and wishes to engage with us. The penultimate is never the ideal; it is a work in progress. Our knowledge of God hopefully increases yet it will never be complete until we are 'face to face'. (1 Corinthians 13:12)

It seems important that this contextualized approach is done in the context of ongoing discussions where issues may be clarified, rather than as a 'hit and run' conversation. Christians who experiment with this approach are on an interesting journey and, who knows, perhaps they and their Buddhist friends may meet God on the way!

Pause for reflection

1. In your opinion, are any of the comparisons we have discussed appropriate to use in an initial conversation about God with a Buddhist? The comparisons were God as the Historical Buddha, the Amitābha Buddha in the Pure Land tradition, the Ādi (Primordial) Buddha, or God as *Dhamma*.

2. Do you think that Hans Küng's critical engagement with possible views of God's personhood and his suggestion that God may better be described as 'transpersonal' rather than 'personal' might make God more readily understood to Buddhists?

Part II

Self

Chapter 5

Buddhist And Christian Understandings Of Self

This chapter examines a number of Buddhist understandings of self and non-self before offering a Christian response. Understanding some of these concepts, particularly the Yogācāra and Zen ideas, will not only help us to engage with 'mind-only' Buddhism, but also the worldviews of some New Age and martial arts practitioners.

In Buddhism, *anatta* (non-self) is one of the three marks of conditioned phenomena. The other two are impermanence and suffering. By suffering, we mean sickness, dissatisfaction, discontent and frustration. Pleasure seldom lasts for long—like everything else, it is impermanent—and we are quickly left looking for another pleasurable experience to take away our dissatisfaction. We may have enjoyed a long and happy relationship, only for that relationship to end, causing significant suffering. Buddhism, as we have seen, helps people understand life's realities and, when we live our lives in the light of reality then our suffering is considerably reduced. Suffering and impermanence are fairly readily understood, but *anatta* is more complex. And so we now turn our attention to some Buddhist understandings of non-self.

What did the Buddha mean by *anatta*?

The nature of self was an important question during the time of the Buddha. The Brahmans sought to explore to *what* or to *whom* the various experiences and parts of a being belong. In the *Upanishads*, the religious texts of the wandering Brahman teachers, the self is viewed as a mysterious entity which cannot be adequately described. It was understood as being related to the Absolute, and this is expressed in the statement '*ātman* is *Brahman*'—the universal self is the Absolute.

There were two widely held views regarding 'self' during this time. First, there was the idea of a self which survived death and lived forever; those who held this position were referred to as 'eternalists'. Second, there were the 'annihilationists', who believed that 'self is an unchanging entity, identical to the body which is destroyed at death'. (Burns, 2003:92) They believed that nothing survived the death experience, and there was no rebirth.

Taking a middle way between these two positions, the Buddha taught that something survives the death experience, but it is not what we understand as a 'self' or a 'soul'. This 'something' was *not the same* as the being who had just passed away *but was not different.* Rather one of the key ideas of the Buddha was dependent origination or conditioned arising (*paṭiccasamuppāda*). Dependent origination is the idea that all things, both physical and mental, come into being as a result of other existing but impermanent conditions. When supporting conditions are removed, that which has arisen in dependence on these conditions will also disappear. The Buddha's position, then, was that there is a constantly changing relationship between different constituent parts or aspects of what comprises sentient existence, and that something of this relationship passes over to the next existence. Indeed, the Buddha's critique of self is directed at all ideas which teach, or even suggest, some sort of 'unchanging self'. One reason for his critique is that these and other ideas are a form of 'clinging', and hold us back from gaining insight into the true nature of existence and enlightenment. The issue is not so much the non-existence or existence of the self, but that when one tries to answer the question of what self is, the unenlightened mind easily gets caught up in false understandings of self. This leads to responding inappropriately to the events of life which, of course, heightens our dissatisfaction. Just as an insistence on there being a stable 'self' is incorrect, so insisting that there is 'no-self' is also misguided. Holding firmly on to views and having aversions to opinions one disagrees with are equally unhelpful.

The Five Aggregates

Imagine that you are out for a walk in the countryside; it is autumn and the leaves are changing colour. After some time you become *conscious* of something in the trees, but it is not yet clear what it is. After some moments, your mind *recognises* this 'something' as a stag. You respond to this recognition with *feelings* of pleasure at being close to this fairly large, majestic animal that normally roams around on higher ground. Last, you engage in *mental activities*. You may reflect on how rare it is to see a stag in that particular area and your action is to get your camera out to take a picture.

This story illustrates how the Five Aggregates of sentient being function together to produce what we understand as a 'personal experience'. The technical term for a component or aggregate is *khandha* (Pali; Sanskrit, *skhanda*.) meaning 'bundle', 'heap', 'aggregate', 'factor' or 'component'.[1] This schema was widely referred to in India at the time of the Buddha, and it was a model he used to demonstrate the way in which we tended to understand what we refer to as 'self'. Buddhists say that this model helps us to view personal experience in terms of impersonal functions and processes. All of this reduces hopes and fears and creates an attitude of non-attachment.

Geoff Hunt, who founded the New Buddha Way fraternity in 2002 has pointed out that the Buddha had no doctrine of the Five Aggregates.[2] Instead, the Buddha was using categories that people of his day readily identified with, and simply invited those who believed that they had a 'soul' or 'real inner me' to look within and observe these aggregates.[3] A person today could well focus on her image and think 'I am

---

[1] A very helpful explanation of the Five Aggregates is Buddha Dharma Education Association (2012). *The Five Aggregates.* http://www.buddhanet.net/funbud14.htm. Also, Sue Hamilton has an interesting discussion of the Five *Khandha*s in S. Hamilton (1997). "Passionlessness in Buddhism". In: *Scottish Journal of Religious Studies* 18.1, pp. 3–23.

[2] In a conversation in Edinburgh on 3rd February 2016. See also *The Five Identifications*, Geoff Hunt, http://www.newbuddhaway.org/.

[3] Hunt prefers the term 'identifications' to 'aggregates'.

my body'. Little wonder she believes that, given the hours she spends in the gym and her strict diet. Another person may be extremely hedonistic and see life simply as an opportunity for experiencing pleasure—'I am my pleasure'.

Hunt's comments challenge us to examine the point the Buddha was making, rather than overly relying on doctrine that has been systematized and passed on by Buddhist teachers. Many books on Buddhism, and especially on Buddhism as it is taught in Asia, do have a strong focus on the Five Aggregates, and so let us return to the story about seeing the stag among the trees! First, *rūpa* ('material shape or form') refers to the material aspect of our living bodies; your body, and the stag you saw in the trees. Material form includes our sensory organs—eye, ear, nose, tongue, body and mind. It also includes our blood pressure, pulse, breathing, temperature and other functions of our body.

The second aggregate or component is *viññāṇa* ('awareness' or 'consciousness').[4] We become aware of thoughts and a particular experience of all the six sense bases: sight, sound, smell, touch, taste and thought. In this case, you became aware or conscious of a shape in the trees. Consciousness is the connection between the mind and the shape or object—in our case, the stag. Wan Petchsongkram (1975:163), a former Thai Buddhist monk, describes awareness as 'the most important of the five *khandhas*, as it is that which passes into a new form of existence after death'. We will consider this in more detail shortly.

---

[4] Buddhism teaching, at least in the Theravadin tradition, mentions the aggregates in the following order: material form, feelings, perceptions, mental activities/will/choices and consciousness. I find it easier to understand these functions by rearranging the order and I hope any Buddhists reading this will not be too hard on me for doing that! Sometimes it is hard to separate the functions e.g. consciousness and recognition. In addition, what comes where depends on the example we use to demonstrate the functions.

The third aggregate is *saññā* ('recognition' or 'perception'). This draws from memory, and is the recognition or labelling of something that we are conscious of. You became aware of the object, which you soon recognized as a stag. Clearly, interpretation or labelling will vary from person to person and will depend on a variety of factors such as gender, age and experience of life. Some people have never seen a stag, are unaware of the existence of such an animal, and are therefore unable to recognize it.

The fourth aggregate is *vedanā* ('feeling' or 'sensation'). This points to a variety of mental activity taking place, much of it in direct response to the various physical stimuli—sight, sound, smell, taste, touch and thought. Harvey (1990:49) comments that 'this is the hedonic tone or "taste" of any experience: pleasant, unpleasant, or neutral. It includes sensations arising from the body and mental feelings of happiness, unhappiness or indifference.' In the example we have just used, you experienced feelings of pleasure at being so close to the stag.

The fifth aggregate is *saṅkhāra*. This refers to mental activities or dispositions which bring about action. Any action may be skillful, unskillful or neutral, and action will 'give shape to character'. (Harvey, 1990:49) Of course, an action may be *no* action—a decision *not* to undertake a certain activity! In our example of the stag, your action was to reach for your camera. This action is hardly life-changing! Yet many of our actions gradually condition us, even to the point of shaping our future. Our mental dispositions have been created by previous choices in this life but also in our countless previous lives. Our previous thoughts have created habits or a particular way of looking at the world. That being said, we can exercise our will and act in a way that is not in keeping with our mental dispositions—change is possible.

According to Buddhist thought, life may be compared to an electrical alternating current (AC) which is constantly pulsating on-off, on-off. Just as the current seems to be flowing constantly but in fact is pulsating on and off, so it is with life. At death, the pulsating process is held in the 'off' position fractionally longer than normal, and consciousness (*viññāṇa*), an impression conditioned by the six senses, flows to another life form that is being brought into being at that point. Death, then, is the end of a set of experiences which progressed in a particular pattern over a lifetime—for example, the pattern of a man which moved progressively from baby, to a boy, to a youth and so on. A traditional Buddhist explanation of this process suggests that the reconfigured pattern, the new life, might well follow a very different pattern from the previous pattern, and so the male human may now be an animal or a god. The (negative) power which causes the flow of consciousness from one life to another comes from the striving, clinging and grasping of the life that has just shut down. Some have suggested that a person's greed, hatred and delusion function as an engine which drives a sentient being from one existence to another. The new life, or reconfigured pattern into which this consciousness flows, is determined by the *karma* connected with the previous lives associated with the trace of consciousness which is being transmitted. Some Buddhists, such as Geoff Hunt, would see this traditional understanding as a metaphysical view, and point out that the Buddha repudiated all such speculation.

The *Culasaccaka Sutta*

The *Culasaccaka Sutta* recounts the story of Saccaka and the Buddha. Saccaka, a teacher of the princes of Vesālī, heard that the Buddha taught the doctrine of the non-self of the Five Aggregrates and went to challenge him. His argument was that, just as a plant depends on the ground for support, so a person may talk about 'self' because his body, experiences, perceptions, choices and awareness are an adequate support for the existence of a 'self'. The Five Aggregates are substantial and just as the ground supports a plant so the Five Aggregates are capable of supporting a 'self'. Thus, we may conclude that there is a self.

The Buddha asked Saccaka if the king of a country holds sovereign power even to the extent of executing one of his subjects, should he so wish. Saccaka affirmed that not only can kings do this, but also elected rulers can as well. Indeed, a king who cannot exercise control over his country cannot call that country 'his'. The Buddha went on to ask Saccaka if he was able to exercise control over his Five Aggregates and Saccaka admitted he was unable to control any of the aggregates. This lack of control indicates that there is insufficient basis for the support of a substantial, permanent self. Someone may cut down a tree for its timber only to discover it is hollow. In a similar way, when one looks inside the human experience, it is discovered to be non-substantial and constantly changing. One needs, therefore, to cut down the tree and look inside to discover what is really inside. In the Buddhist tradition, this is done through meditation. The Buddha encouraged Saccaka to do this and indicated that when he did he would discover that 'mine' was really 'not mine' and 'I' was really 'not I'. Indeed, what one refers to as self is hardly worth the designation of 'self'.

Thus, with 'skilful means', the Buddha pointed out to Saccaka that a genuine or real self is something over which one should have full control. 'Self', by definition, should describe a person and belong to a particular person; if it really is his 'self', then that person should be able to exercise control over it. There is, therefore, no self, because we are unable to control the actions and reactions that are constantly arising and falling in our five 'bundles' or *khandhas*. Our 'bundles' have no leader, no guide and no inner controller. If the goal of our path is freedom from suffering, as it is in Buddhism, then we will learn to respond appropriately to change or impermanence, and this will lead to a reduction in our suffering. After all, why should a 'person' who is in constant flux hold tightly onto something which is constantly changing?

So according to the Buddha, there is no evidence for an independent, fixed, substantive self. It is not found in any one of the aggregates. The Five Aggregates added up together do not produce a self, they only add up to 'something' we fleetingly experience. All one may say is that the Five Aggregates are interconnected and constantly changing. One aggregate is, because the other aggregates are. Of course, we use the word 'self' to refer to the current state of our ever-changing psychophysical personality. That 'self' will have a name, a social network, be part of a family and probably have a role in the world of work. But this must not trick us into thinking that all of this constitutes a stable, unchanging self; the reality is, we are constantly changing. Our constitute parts or 'bundles' impact each another, and are conditioned by that which lies beyond us in ways which we are not always able to control. Rupert Gethin (1998:139) makes the important point: "Language and the fact that experiences are somehow connected fool us into thinking that there is an 'I' apart from and behind changing experiences." Indeed, in the Western philosophical tradition, Kant, Hume and others have said something similar.

Unfortunately, we cannot use this idea to avoid our responsibilities. When my daughter gets yet another parking ticket placed on the windscreen of her car and argues that there is only a constantly changing set of experiences and no real person who committed the parking offence, this will probably not allow her off the hook! Indeed, if the traffic warden were Buddhist he would be quick to say that the person who has been handed the ticket currently exists through dependence on the one who parked the car illegally, and the person who will eventually have to pay the fine will come into being as a set of experiences emerging from the one who is disagreeing with the decision!

The Buddha did not completely deny the existence of soul or self, but indicated that he could not locate it. He taught that nothing in the human condition—that is, the Five Aggregates—occurs independently, and in this sense all beings are without a 'self'. He believed that it was meaningless to think that a self existed independently of the Five Aggregates. Within these aggregates, he did not see a self that was anything other than connections between them at any one particular point in time. The function of non-self teaching is not to establish a doctrine, but simply to eliminate self-interest and cultivate a lifestyle of non-attachment. In turn, this will lead to liberation from suffering. Many Christians do not appreciate the purpose of this teaching and get caught up in a philosophical discussion, usually vigorously defending the existence of a soul or spirit, an entity that survives the death experience.

The Buddha frequently used the metaphor of fire in his teaching, usually with a negative connotation. The *khandha*s may be considered as bundles of firewood which are constantly ablaze, until such time as our cravings are extinguished. This extinction of cravings is referred to as '*nibbāna* (a cooling off) of the aggregates'. That is to say, the components of body, experiences, perceptions, choices, and awareness are still there but they are no longer on fire. The fires of greed, hatred and delusion have been extinguished by the person who has followed the Noble Eightfold Path at the higher level. In the Theravādin tradition the person at this stage is referred to as an *arahat*. When the *arahat* passes away, he enters '*nibbāna* without the Five Aggregates'. The Buddha was often asked about the existence of the *arahat* in *nibbāna*. He replied that the *arahat* does not exist, he does not not exist, he does not both exist and not exist, and he does not neither exist and neither not exist. Rather than describe the nature of this existence, the Buddha taught that we may all experience *nibbāna* by following the Noble Eight Fold Path at the higher level.

The 'Chariot Story'

The 'Chariot Story' is well known within the Buddhist tradition. It concerns King Milinda, or Menander who ruled over an area in South India in the middle of the second century BCE, and Nāgasena, the famous monk philosopher. One tradition suggests that the king converted to Buddhism through Nāgasena's teaching. When the king met Nāgasena for the first time he asked the monk his name. The monk replied 'Sire, I am known as Nāgasena, yet that is only a name and a designation; there is really no person.' The monk is simply making the point that he is not an unchanging, permanent entity. The king goes on to ask questions such as: if you are not a person, how can we give you alms and how can you use these alms? Who is it, if it is not you, who is practising meditation? The king goes on to ask Nāgasena, 'if you tell people to call you Nāgasena, who are these people actually addressing?' In respone Nāgasena asks the king to show him his chariot. He then goes on to ask the king: what actually is the chariot, is it the wheels, the flagstaff or the platform? Nāgasena makes the point that it is all these components which have come together at a particular point in time, and only for a certain period of time, which create the 'chariot'. The chariot exists as a name, or designation. The nun Vajira is attributed with the following saying:

> Just as when the parts are rightly set
> the word 'chariot' is spoken
> so when there are the *khandas*
> it is the convention to say 'being'.
> (Milinda's Questions 2:5-8)

This story flags up the inappropriateness of identifying the coming together of the Five Aggregates at one brief moment in time as a 'permanent self'. Although we commonly use the term 'self', according to Buddhism we should not think of it as meaning that which is unchanging, independent or permanent.

A belief in a self which needs to have certain experiences before it may be content will always be attached to pleasure-seeking, and so much of life is spent looking forward to the next pleasurable experience. This, along with our clinging, striving and grasping bring only suffering, while letting go of both clinging and aversions bring peace (*sukha*).

But is the purpose and practice of selfless living solely in order to be enlightened actually just a deluded form of religious self-absorption? A Buddhist in the Mahāyāna tradition would point out that the quest for liberation goes hand in hand with helping other beings reach enlightenment and becoming emancipated from suffering. And so the taking of the *bodhisattva* vow in Mahāyāna Buddhism means that the aspirant focuses on the well-being of others, not just his or her own quest for enlightenment. Indeed, the *bodhisattva* may undertake an unskilful act, generating negative karmic consequences, in order to relieve the suffering of another being.

Madhayamaka understanding of self

The understanding of non-self in the Mahāyāna tradition resonates with what has been said so far, but it goes beyond these understandings—according to Theravāda thinking, a step too far beyond! Nāgārjuna (CE 150-250), a philosopher and monk from South India and regarded as the founder of what is referred to as the Madhyamaka, or Śūnyatā-vada, school viewed everything and everyone as empty. The *dhammas*, the building blocks of everything are empty; they have no discrete essence. They are not self-contained because what they depend upon for their existence conditions them. Certainly there is something to be experienced, and so we cannot deny the building blocks of that particular experience, object or person. But that existence is not substantial. As Harvey (1990:97) comments, 'what we experience does not exist in an absolute sense, but only, in a relative way, as a passing phenomenon'. And so we can see that everything lacks an inherent nature; 'self' and the nature of all things is non-nature. Nothing is self-existent and everything is interconnected.

The Yogācāra understanding of self

The Yogācāra tradition, and the Zen tradition which it informs, is important as we try to understand marshal arts and the philosophy that underpins some forms of Buddhist spirituality. Yogācāra, an Indian Mahāyāna Buddhist school, was founded by the brothers Asanga and Vasubandhu. This fraternity is also referred to as Mind-Only or Cittā-mātra. Asaṅga was born in the fourth century CE into a Brahmin family in modern Peshawar. He was the eldest of three brothers and a monk in the Mahisasaka tradition of early Buddhism.[5] He received teaching from Maitreyanatha, who was either a human teacher or the future Buddha Maitreya. Either way, Asaṅgha was provided with a series of texts that were collected under the name of Maitreyanatha. Quickly converting to Mahāyāna as a result of this encounter, Asanga began composing texts in his own name, founded the Yogācāra school of Buddhism, and converted his brother Vasubandhu who, by that time, had developed a reputation as one of the eminent teachers of the Sarvāstivadin fraternity.[6]

The Yogācāra viewed the true nature of everything as a construction of the mind. According to Harvey (1990:106), "[I]n the Yogācāra, the role of the mind in constructing the world is so emphasized that all concepts of an external physical reality are rejected: the perceived world is seen as 'representation only' (*vijnapti-mātra*) or 'thought only' (*citta-mātra*)." In Buddhist meditation, a visualised object appears real. Despite its vividness, however, it exists only in the meditator's mind. If a meditator, in a state of awareness, is almost convinced that the object is real, how much more might a person be deluded about reality when he is generally unmindful.

---

[5] The origins of this group may go back to the Second Buddhist Council held at Vesali some 30 years before the accession of the Emperor Asoka. In his *Indian Buddhism*, AK Warder (2000:280) says that this fraternity established itself in Sri Lanka and eventually was absorbed into the Theravāda tradition. Certainly the ideas of this fraternity were similar to that of Theravāda beliefs.

[6] The Sarvāstivāda fraternity had its own canon of Scripture as well as monastic rules and own ordination lineage. Paul Williams (2000:13) comments that this group had a particular interest in ontological issues. It distinguished between how *dharmas* (building blocks) exist and the way that things created out of these *dharmas* exist. They also believed that the *arhat* could regress from his enlightened state from time to time. The Sarvāstivadins were also referred to as Pan-Realists. The fraternity became a dominant non-Mahāyāna school in North India and flourished under the patronage of Kaniska I who ruled late first or early second century CE.

The Yogācāra school addressed some of the philosophical issues associated with emptiness and 'thought-only', and a system was advanced which brought Mahāyāna ideas together. These major philosophical ideas are sometimes referred to as the 'third turning of the wheel of the *Dharma*'. These are higher teachings than the 'first turning'—the Four Noble Truths—and the 'second turning', the emptiness teaching of the wisdom texts of the Mahāyāna tradition. The mind-only teaching of Yogācāra is shared by the Zen school of thought and we now turn to see how the mind functions in these traditions as well as their understanding of 'self'.

Some understandings of self in Zen Buddhism

The object of Zen is to gain a new perspective (*satori*), or to see one's true nature (*kenshō*).[7] The famous Japanese Zen scholar DT Suzuki (1870-1966) comments that to enter into the truth of Zen, there must be *satori*; there must be a general upheaval which destroys traditional views and reviews the old things from a 'hitherto undreamed of angle'. A classical Zen position takes the view that only mind exists. Through your senses, you are conscious of what you believe to be real. This reality is, in fact, a dream existing as a creation of your mind, and it only exists in your mind. Immanuel Kant (1724-1804) taught that the only thing one can know is the contents of one's own consciousness, what he called *phenomena*. One cannot know the things in the world external to consciousness, or *noumena*. Kant, however, believed that the experience inside the mind is in response to stimuli existing out with the mind.

We now move on to explore the levels of consciousness or functions of the mind. The first five levels are the five senses of

---

[7] Please refer to the appendix for explanations of *satori* and *kenshō*.

sound, sight, smell, taste and touch. The sixth consciousness is 'thought consciousness' and this is everything one thinks or feels. One sees something but it is 'thought consciousness' which responds with a feeling of disgust or anticipation. In Zen, these thoughts are not responses to an external world because the so-called 'external world' is understood as a fabrication of the mind.

The seventh level of consciousness is the 'spectator-consciousness'. This level of consciousness is the spectator of everything that takes place in the first six levels. It is the ego or 'I' that says 'I smell the curry', 'I see the bus', 'I feel the wind', and so on. 'Spectator-consciousness' does not observe itself. It is, however, the unseen observer of the contents of the mind's first six levels of consciousness. Our 'spectator-consciousness' thinks that what is learnt from the six levels of consciousness reflects an external reality. The Yogācāra and Zen fraternities, however, would know that what is seen is real *only* in the mind. Buddhists may well compare life and the passing of the years to corks bobbing around in a constantly moving, ever changing stream. The Yogācāra and Zen traditions go one step further and say that there are no corks, there is only the stream! The stream may run into a river and then into the sea where waves will eventually break up on a beach and the water will be absorbed into the atmosphere, only to condense out as water on the earth or back into the sea.

There is an eight and final function of the mind. The Japanese term *Araya-shiki* transliterates the Sanskrit *ālaya-vijñāna*, the 'stored-up consciousness'. This may be described as a reservoir where our yet to be experienced thoughts, sensations and emotions are kept. Indeed, all karmic seed is to be found in this realm and from here signals are transmitted to the other seven levels of consciousness. Harvey (1990:108) refers to the karmic seed when he remarks:

In any situation we only really notice what our mind is attuned to perceive, be this something that interests us, threatens us, excites us or disgusts us... What we perceive is clearly related to our nature, which is the product, amongst other things, of our previous actions.

The 'stored-up consciousness' is like a reel of film that has not yet being projected onto the screen but in due course it will wind its way through the lens and be seen by the 'film-watcher'. Callaway, 1976:31-51 helpfully uses the example of a film projector to explain the different levels of consciousness. It may be diagrammed as follows.

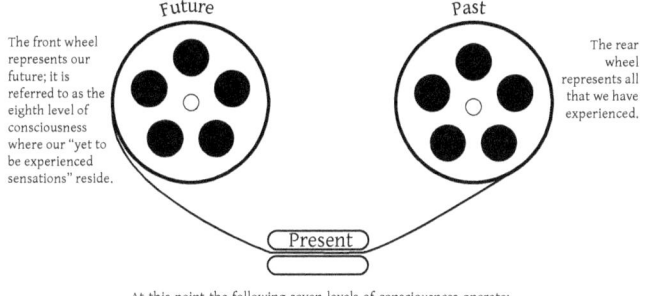

At this point the following seven levels of consciousness operate: *sound*, *sight*, *smell*, *touch* and *taste* (five senses). At the sixth level (consciousness) a *choice* is made. At the seventh level (spectator or observer consciousness), all that has taken place in the previous six levels of consciousness is *observed*.

Figure 5.1: Eight functions of the mind according to Yogācāra / Zen thought

A further reflection on 'mind-only' ideas

Two novice Zen monks are talking together on a windy day. One says 'The leaves on the trees are moving.' The other novice replies 'It is the wind that is moving.' The master overhears the conversation and interrupts by saying 'It is not the leaves which move, it is not the wind, it is the mind.' In the film *The Matrix*, Spoon Boy says to Neo, 'Don't try and bend the spoon; that is impossible. Instead, only try to realise the truth.' Neo asks 'What truth?' and Spoon Boy replies 'There is no spoon.' I think if Callaway were to read this, he would say that in order for Spoon Boy to bend the spoon he would first have to access the 'front reel of the projector' (stored-up consciousness) and adjust the spoon's image so it is perceived to be bent. But how will Spoon Boy adjust the pictures that are already created and waiting to be experienced by the spectator?

You may recognise the two examples above as a form of metaphysical idealism, or immaterialism—the idea that mind is the ultimate foundation of all reality. Remember the classic riddle: Does a tree falling in the forest make a sound if there is nobody there to hear it fall? My guess is that most of us would affirm that the falling tree would make a noise even although no one was present to hear it fall. Metaphysical idealism, however, takes the view that ordinary objects are ideas which we perceive and this perception creates their presence: without a mind perceiving the tree, how can it exist!

George Berkeley (1685-1753), a philosopher and Anglican bishop thought it was strange that we think all objects have an existence *apart* from our perception of them. After all, what are these objects but something that we perceive in our minds? How can any object exist unless it is perceived in someone's mind? Berkeley's position was "I am perceived, therefore I am". So, to continue with the example of the tree, Berkeley would have argued that if there is no one present to perceive the tree, it exists because it is perceived by God. Berkeley understood that God perceived everything, including our perceiving minds. This continuous act of perception on the part of God, according to Berkeley, assures our existence. Berkeley went on to say that God puts some ideas into our mind; he terms these 'ideas of sense'. These ideas could be the sensing of this book in your hands, its size, shape and weight. These ideas come from out with our mind and are created by the existence of another mind; Berkeley calls this Mind 'God'.

We could develop Berkeley's ideas. For example, if something is in the mind of God then it exists, but if 'something' does not exist in the mind of God then it does not exist. One of the central themes of the Christian faith is that if a person acknowledges their unskilful actions (sins) and looks to God for forgiveness, then that will be granted. And this is exactly what those who experience a sense of remorse and shame as a result of inappropriate behaviour need to hear. In the Christian Scriptures, God is depicted as saying of his wayward people, 'For I will forgive their wickedness and remember their sins no more.' (Jeremiah 31:34) These sinful actions no longer exist in the mind of God because of a person's confession of sin and Christ's taking on himself the punishment for that sin.

Puggalavādin understandings of self

Exposure to other world views, speculation on what the Buddha really meant and philosophical reflection on his practical message produced new understandings and perhaps also misunderstanding of his teachings. The Madhyamaka, Yogācāra and Zen traditions are examples of this especially in the area of the nature of self. We turn our attention briefly to the Puggalavādins, also known as the Personalism school of Buddhism, which emerged around 250BCE. According to Harvey (1990:85), by the seventh century CE a quarter of Indian monks belonged to this fraternity. We do not know a lot about their belief system apart from what their opponents said about them. They were a group of five early schools of Buddhism who came to be distinguished by their view of the reality of the self.[8] Amongst other things, this fraternity used the illustration of a clay model of an ox in comparison to a live ox. If a person were to intentionally break the model, this would be very different from killing a real ox. The Puggalavādins reasoned that the difference between a clay model and the real ox is that which constitutes life, has a substantiality all of its own, and constitutes a subtle self.

This fraternity also used the analogy of fire and fuel and argued that the relationship of the fire to the fuel was the same as that of a self to the Five Bundles. A fire is described in terms of its fuel—for instance, a wood or straw fire. The fire is not the same as the fuel; it cannot exist without the fuel, and it is something more than the fuel. In a similar way the person is not the Five Bundles, cannot exist without the bundles, and is something greater than the bundles. This 'something greater' is what constitutes personhood. The Puggalavāda fraternity believed in the permanence of a person in this life and from life to life until passing over into enlightenment. There is, they reasoned, a person who experiences life moment by moment and benefits when he follows the teachings of the Buddha. The Buddha is also a 'person' who was born into this world for the happiness of other 'people'.

The Puggalavādins also used the concept of memory to argue for personhood. If there is a constantly changing self, then how is it possible that we may remember the details of a one hour conversation with someone else some 10 years after the event? The fleeting nature of interaction between the Five Bundles and the many millions of states which passed since

---

[8] For further information on this fraternity, see 'Puggalavāda (Pudgalavada) Buddhist Philosophy' in *the Internet Encyclopaedia of Philosophy* by Leonard Priestly, available at http://www.iep.utm.edu/p/pudgalav.htm.

the conversation took place point to something continuous underpinning these moments.⁹ The Puggalavādins believed that this act of memory required a moment-to-moment continuity which they suggested was a form of self.

A summary of the main understandings of self within Buddhism

The Puggalavādin support for some kind of self was viewed by some as 'not proper Buddhism' and as a compromise with Jainism and Hinduism. Certainly the Puggalavādin tradition is closer to the Christian understanding of self than Zen and Yogācāra perspectives. True, we are like Saccaka in that we are not really in control of ourselves; sometimes life brings us into the experience of that reality, and we understand something of our own vulnerability. Our aspirations and interests are in flux and many people come to appreciate that striving for achievement and status often does not bring any lasting satisfaction. There is little point, then, in an ever changing person striving after something which will not bring enduring contentment. Elizabeth Harris (2005:40) is surely right when she sums up the counter-cultural message of the Buddha as 'Change the way you construct your idea of self. Release yourself from promoting, protecting and pampering an "I" that in reality doesn't exist.' Charlene Burns (2003:96) reminds us of the purpose of the idea of no-self: 'The point of learning to

---

⁹ Yandell and Netland (2009:153) comment that the fleeting nature of such states is indicated by 'the Buddhist saying that more than sixty-five come and go in the time it takes a strong man to snap his fingers'. Assuming that this is true then 234,000 'personless' but connected states passed during the one hour conversation that we mentioned. If the conversation was recalled by the person some 10 years after the conversation then 315.36 million such states would have passed!

release attachment to the idea of selfhood is to be capable of practising compassion for all living beings.' Compassion for others is an essential feature of both Buddhism and Christianity.

Humans as non-self but God as self: a conversation starter?

At the beginning of the Christian Scriptures (Exodus 3) there is an interesting account of Moses' encounter with God in the desert, some 800 to 900 years before the birth of the Buddha. If we think of humankind being non-self, could we not view God as self (*atta*), or indeed the great self (*mahāatta*), since He is not subject to the changes of *saṃsāra* and is beyond the nature of conditioned arising?

God speaks out of a bush which kept on burning, which attracted the attention of Moses. He indicates that He has seen the sufferings of the Jews under an oppressive Egyptian regime and was going to liberate them. Moses, whose own attempts at freeing the Jews from their oppression resulted in his running away to the desert, wonders if this liberation is possible. He shrewdly asks God what His name is: an indirect way of asking about the probability of a successful outcome! God discloses His name as 'I AM WHO I AM,' from which we get 'Jehovah', one of God's names. Moses is not interested in the sound of the name, or even the name itself but whether the one who speaks from the burning bush is *able* to do as he promised. 'I am', or 'own nature' (God) can liberate the Jewish people despite the overwhelming odds. This unfettered power is the nature of the one who may be referred to as the greatself (*mahāatta*) whose existence is not predicated on any cause and stands in contrast to the limitations of human existence.

Toward an understanding of the Christian view of self

Two areas of interest in the discussion on self are 'at what point does a new life have spirit?' and 'should we think of spirit, soul and body or, more simply, spirit/soul and body?' Regarding the origin of a person's spirit, there are two basic positions. First, there is creationism, the view that God creates the spirit of each human and implants it into the developing child. This could occur when the egg is fertilized, or implanted in the uterus, or possibly when the foetus is viable or even when the baby draws its first breath at birth. An implication of the creation position may well be that abortion and post-fertilization contraception may be acceptable if the spirit has not yet been granted to the emerging life. Traducianism, on the other hand, states that the spirit of the child comes from the father and mother and occurs when the egg is fertilized. Thus, the spirit of the new life originates and develops with the conception and growth of the unborn child. The traducian position fits in well with the widely held Christian position that a person inherits a sinful nature from his or her parents. This concept of 'original sin', of course, does not resonate with Buddhist thinking which favours original purity and the eventual return to our true (Buddha) nature. Those who hold to the traducian perspective have less ethical leeway on the abortion issue than the creationists. This is because the traducianists understand that spirit is given at conception, and so post-fertilization contraception and abortion is considered to be taking human life.[10]

---

[10] See S. Grenz (2000). *Theology for the Community of God*. Grand Rapids, Michigan: W.B. Eerdmans, chapter 6, for a helpful discussion of human nature, including the origin of soul/spirit and the tripartite or bipartite nature and image of God.

The second issue to raise here is what constitutes the nature of humankind. A tripartite position argues for a triad of body, soul and spirit. While the Christian Scriptures sometimes mention this triad in the one sentence, it may be best to understand this as the author's attempt to flag up our various functions of thinking, decision making, as well as our attitudes to God and others. The bipartite model conflates the inner, non-material functions of soul and spirit into 'spirit'; the point here being that something survives the death experience apart from the human body and, whatever that is, it is dependent on the power of God.

Regardless of whether we take a tripartite or bipartite approach, a key aspect of the human dimension is what is referred to as the image of God, the *imago Dei*. Humankind is created in the image of God. It is not necessary, then, to make an image of God, because he has already populated the world with images of Himself! When we respect the image of God in others by treating them with dignity, then we honour God. Conversely, when we look down on others we not only belittle them but we also belittle God. We find reference to the image of God in the creation narrative, 'Then God said let us make man in our image [*tselem*], in our likeness [*demuth*]' (Genesis 1:26). The Hebrew words *tselem* and *demuth* are, more or less, interchangeable; they function as a literary device—one meaning through two descriptions.[11]

Clearly, it is in relationship with God that the image of God shines out and develops. Leslie Newbigin makes this point rather well when he comments:

---

[11] In an unpublished essay entitled *In What Ways and to What Extent is God Present to Non-Believers and How Might this Influence our Approach to Faith Sharing*, 2014 Geraint Williamson points out that the early Church Fathers believed that the image of God is evidenced in everyone, but *likeness* to God was lost to humankind at the Fall.

> On a still and cloudless night we may see the image of the moon in the water of a lake. So long as the water is unruffled by the wind, and the moon is not covered by cloud, the image will shine out – clear and beautiful. But if the cloud comes between the moon and the earth the image will disappear, or if the water is ruffled by wind the image will be scattered and distorted. Thus the image of the moon in the water does not belong to the water. The image depends upon a certain relationship between the moon and the water. If this relationship is broken, the image is distorted.
>
> (Quoted in Silva, 1975:82)

In addition to a person opening him or herself up to the influence of God—what we may call a vertical component—there is also a horizontal component. The capacity for community and relationship is a significant aspect of what it means to be created in the image of God. Just as God has always existed in an eternal community of Father, Son and Holy Spirit, so we are designed to live in relationship with others as well as with God. Indeed, it is in this horizontal component, the communities in which we work and play, that the rough edges are knocked off. Many Christians believe that the image of God within humankind was severally distorted by Adam's disobedience of God. Yet this image of God has not been obliterated. Indeed, after the flood, God said to Noah, 'Whoever sheds the blood of man, by man shall his blood be shed; for in the image of God has God made man.' (Genesis 9:6) According to this particular Scripture, there is sufficient 'likeness' to God remaining in humankind to constitute the death penalty to those who attack that part of God's creation which most resembles himself.

Part of being made in the image of God means we represent God and his interests and values, on earth. Grudem (1994:443) states that to the original hearers, Genesis 1:26 would have meant 'Let us make man to be *like* us and to *represent* us'. This representing of God on earth is a key function of humankind, and this responsibility is sometimes referred to as the 'cultural mandate'. The first humans were given delegated sovereignty over God's earthly creation and were to care for and bring out the best in creation, functioning as God's vice-regents on earth (Genesis 1:28). The earth with all its resources is entrusted to humankind for our use and stewardship. Distribution of wealth, the balance of nature, the functions of the institutions of marriage, family and government, peace keeping, reconciliation and the liberation of the oppressed all fall within the cultural mandate. We often find the call to mirror God by acting in socially responsible ways in the New Testament. For example, John the Baptist was reminding his listeners of the cultural mandate and all that it entailed when he said in Luke 3:11, 'The man with two tunics should share with him who has none, and the one who has food should do the same.' In Matthew 22:7-39, Jesus talks about loving our neighbour as our self. Because we are created in the image of God, we have both a capacity and responsibility to act as God's representatives on earth.

A perspective from St Paul

The Apostle Paul who according to tradition was martyred outside Rome around 66CE, was also known as Saul up until the time he became a follower of Jesus. He was an up-and-coming Jewish rabbi who had studied under Gamaliel, a highly respected teacher of the Law (*Dhamma*) and a member of the

Pharisees, the strictest of all Jewish religious fraternities. Saul demonstrated zeal and commitment to God as well as rigorously observing the Mosaic Law and all the oral add-ons which surrounded it. He dismissed the claim that Jesus of Nazareth was the only saviour (messiah) sent from God. According to Hawthorne (1983:134):

> Paul harried the church, only he did so, on his own confession with a maniacal zealousness that brought prison and death to innocent men and women of the Way as people who belonged to the church of Jesus Christ.

Saul was present at the stoning to death of Stephen, a deacon of the early church. (Acts 7:58) In addition, he successfully applied to the high priest for permission to arrest followers of Jesus in Damascus. (Acts 9:1-2) It was on his journey to Damascus that Saul had a vision of Jesus, and, after a three day period of blindness, was baptised as a follower of Jesus Christ. Reviewing his life from the confines of a prison cell almost three decades later, Paul concludes that his Jewish ancestry, theological education, membership of an ultra-strict religious fraternity and, of course, his zealous activities, all things he once considered profitable, are a 'loss' compared with what he has gained. (Philippians 3:7) Paul indicates that he has gained a relationship with Christ where his earlier rigorous keeping of the Mosaic Law has been replaced by a trust in the righteousness of Jesus Christ for a right standing with God.

This different approach to life is expressed cryptically in a letter which Paul wrote to churches he and others helped to establish in Turkey. In Galatians 2:20, we read:

> I have been crucified with Christ and I no longer live,
> but Christ lives in me.
> The life I live in the body,
> I live by faith in the Son of God,
> who loved me and gave himself for me.

Who is living? Is it Paul, Christ, *both* Paul and Christ, or *neither* Paul nor Christ? Who is 'self' in this verse? Paul is trying to make the point that self-righteousness and self-effort have both gone. This is replaced by a crucified self, a life lived in partnership with Christ. Paul states that he and Christ are both alive despite both having been crucified; indeed Christ lives in him. It is fair to say that by this Paul means that his old aspirations, which were pursued ruthlessly and caused intense suffering to others, have been replaced by selfless and God-focused activity. We may presume that Christ's values and intentions now motivate Paul. Indeed, he lives his 'crucified' life by trust (Pali *saddhā*) in the one who was crucified for him. Paul uses this cruel instrument of Roman execution to describe his reorientation of self and his relationship with Jesus Christ who he had previously cursed. He is telling this story within the community of those who view Jesus Christ as God. Many were beginning to go back to a dependency on law-keeping as the source of their right standing before God. Paul, as we have seen, had been a rigorous keeper of the Jewish law. The Pharisee fraternity in which he was an upwardly-mobile teacher rigorously attempted to keep the 600 or so laws of the Jewish tradition. It was popularly believed that if anyone was able to perfectly keep these laws for one day then God would send his Messiah to deliver the Jewish people from their enemies.

Paul, as a result of his dramatic encounter with Jesus while on his way to arrest followers of Jesus, was dead to rule-keeping. He had come to discover that a lifestyle based on observing an excessively rigorous legal code produced self-righteousness when the precepts were kept and despondency when they were broken. Paul is liberated from a religious box-ticking practice carried out to gain acceptance from God and other religious people. He was represented on the cross by Christ, which is why Paul says he was crucified with Christ. Christ who was dead now lives in Paul, and Paul who died with Christ now lives in Christ. This master-devotee relationship shapes Paul into someone who is more Christ-like. This mystical union or transformative relationship between a master and a devotee is not lost on a Buddhist. In some Buddhist meditative practices, the qualities of the *bodhisattva* or teacher become those of the follower.

Longenecker (1990:92) writes that 'crucifixion with Christ implies not only death to the jurisdiction of the Mosaic Law (v 19), but also death to the jurisdiction of one's own ego'. First, there is the move away from self-righteousness to the righteousness of Jesus Christ. At the end of the passage from Galatians which we quoted earlier Paul writes, '[I]f righteousness could be gained through the law, Christ died for nothing.' On the surface, the reason Christ died was the animosity of the religious leaders of Palestine toward a young man who challenged the religious practice of the time. The deeper purpose of the crucifixion of the Son of God is the removal of what separates us from God. Commenting on the Christian understanding of the crucifixion, DT Suzuki (1957:116) writes 'In the first sense it symbolizes the destruction of the individual ego, while in the second it stands for the doctrine of vicarious atonement whereby all our sins are atoned for by making Christ die for them.' The destruction of the ego, or at least an admission of the inadequacy of self, is a kind of Christian *satori*, an acquiring of a new way of looking at things.

Second, there is the replacement of self-dependency with dependence on Jesus Christ. That is, the giving up of the notion of the adequacy of self-power (*jiriki* in Japanese Buddhism) to a relationship with Christ where his power is both sought and found (*tariki*). For Paul, to participate in Christ's death is to share in Christ's resurrection. If Christ's presence produces within Paul a power which conquers death, then that presence is surely an empowering one. Paul needed strength to endure a catalogue of opposition and obstacles in his work of planting and strengthening churches. In defending his missionary practice against criticism from some teachers who were causing problems to the young church in Corinth, Paul writes:

> I have worked much harder [than these false teachers who claim apostolic authority], been in prison more frequently, been flogged more severely, and been exposed to death again and again. Five times I received from the Jews the forty lashes minus one. Three times I was beaten with rods, once I was stoned, three times I was shipwrecked, I spent a night and a day in the open sea, I have been constantly on the move. I have been in danger from rivers, in danger from bandits, in danger from my own countrymen, in danger from Gentiles; in danger in the city, in danger in the country, in danger at sea; and in danger from false brothers. I have laboured and toiled and have often gone without sleep; I have known hunger and thirst and have often gone without food; I have been cold and naked. Besides everything else, I face daily the pressure of my concern for all the churches. Who is weak, and I do not feel weak? Who is led into sin, and I do not inwardly burn?

(2 Corinthians 11:23-29, written around 57CE)

Sourcing, or plugging in to 'other power', does not mean lack of effort. The Christian path is not an easy option, as real cost is involved. At any rate, someone beyond our 'self' is involved with us, so one cannot call this 'self-effort'. Yet in discussing faith with Buddhists, some Christians too readily give the impression that faith and trust in God does away with discipline and effort. Paul faced many physical challenges; some arose by dint of being a traveller in the first century, while others are the result of his religious convictions and evangelistic activities. He also mentions his struggles 'against the rulers, against the authorities, against the powers of this dark world and against the spiritual forces of evil in the heavenly realm'. (Ephesians 6:12) In this verse, the 'rulers' and 'authorities' are most likely a reference to the dictatorial political and military forces of the Roman empire. The reference to 'powers of this dark world and the spiritual forces of evil' could be understood as unseen spiritual forces hostile to the advance of the message that we may be reconciled to God through trust in Jesus Christ.

Pause for reflection

1. You are asked to give a talk on *Buddhist Understandings of the Self*. Write out your main points.

2. A lecturer at a seminary for Buddhist monks invites you to come along and give a lecture on the *Christian View of How We Might Reach our True Potential*. What ideas would you wish to get across in your lecture?

Part III

Salvation

Chapter 6

Karma And The Transfer Of Merit As A Redemptive Analogy

Liberation in Buddhism: Salvation in Christianity

The Buddha's ability to find the way lost to humankind and to motivate others to take it means, at least from a Buddhist perspective, that there *is* a journey which will lead to liberation from suffering. Buddhadasa (1967:113) comments that 'the real redeemer is none other than the traveller himself'. As we have seen, Buddhists—at least in theory—tend to focus more on the *Dhamma*, what the Buddha discovered and taught, rather than the Buddha himself. And so we see, that the Buddha is not technically a saviour; he simply points the way to liberation. Yet Brinkman (2009:87) draws out the way in which some Buddhists perceive the Buddha as a saviour figure, when he writes, 'a way became visible in his life as in no other life, and to that extent that life also includes an aspect of granting salvation. On that basis he is also revered personally.'

Certainly the journey from selfish nature to selflessness cannot be taken on someone else's behalf; the responsibility for moving from a nature which causes suffering for self and others, to being a selfless person, can only be taken by that person. But at the same time, we need to realise that there is another aspect to the Buddha's insistence on 'self being the refuge of self'. The Buddha taught self-reliance because he was afraid that reliance on a teacher would result in further suffering, not liberation. Everyone is subject to change and, as time goes by, we may become disappointed with our teachers. It is better, then, to take responsibility for our own journey.

Access to the Christian way is not earned by one's efforts, but the Christian way does make moral demands upon the person who follows it. These demands are not viewed by Christians as an act of making merit, but rather doing good out of a sense of gratitude to God. Attachment to things is discouraged because it holds a person back from useful service of others and from encountering God in a deep way. In Mark 10:17-22, we read of a rich young man who had kept the precepts since boyhood and who went to see Jesus for advice. After paying his respects to Jesus, the wandering teacher, the man asks what he must do to inherit eternal life. The Jewish understanding was that there would be life in the 'age to come' for those who had lived a good life, once 'this age' passed away. Those who were righteous would be raised to life and have a part in the 'age to come', never to die again. The young man clearly aspired to this, and Jesus mentions some of the commandments. It is impossible to ignore the fact that four of the Five Buddhist Precepts are mentioned. The final precept of refraining from the use of intoxicants is not referred to here, although drunkenness is condemned elsewhere in Scripture. What Jesus adds in terms of the Five Precepts is refraining from defrauding, perhaps a reference to holding back the wages of employees or disadvantaging poor people in other ways. (Nineham, quoted by Evans, 2001-03:96) Honouring one's father and mother is also added. This is the fifth of the Ten Commandments of the Christian faith and indeed, a core virtue in Buddhism.

Jesus discerns that the fetter holding this man back from eternal life is his attachment to his wealth. He tells the man, 'Go sell everything you have and give to the poor and then you will have treasure in heaven. Then come, follow me.' Two actions are called for here. The second, following Jesus, is not possible for this young man without the first, giving up an attachment to something other than God. Jesus, as would any good teacher, challenges the notion that we can have what we want *and* what holds us back from achieving that! The call of Jesus to the young man reminds us of the words of the Buddha to those who wished to follow: *ehi bikkhu* or 'come, monk'.

Buddhism recognizes that acquiring wealth is not, of itself, evil. The critical issues relate to how riches are acquired, used, and of the owner's attachment to wealth. A number of the Buddha's lay disciples were wealthy, such as the banker and businessman Anathapindika, who constructed the Jetavana monastery at Sāvatthī in NE India where the Buddha spent the last 20 years of his life. In one conversation with him, the Buddha pointed out that there was absolutely nothing wrong with being contented with wealth, providing the wealth was gained lawfully, and shared with others:

> In the case where this enjoyer of sense pleasures seeks after wealth lawfully, not arbitrarily, and in

> so doing makes himself happy and cheerful, and
> also shares his wealth with others and does meri-
> torious deeds therewith, and further makes use of
> it without greed and longing, without infatuation,
> and is not heedless of the danger or blind to his
> own salvation—in such a case he is praiseworthy
> on four counts. (*Aṅguttara Nikāya*, 5:181, Tr. FL
> Woodward 1972)

The well known Thai scholar monk Phra Rajavaramuni (1990:11)—also known as Phra Payutto—notes that 'a true Buddhist lay person not only seeks wealth lawfully and spends it for the good but also enjoys freedom, not being attached to it, infatuated with or enslaved by that wealth'.

The moral rigour of the young man we have been discussing was insufficient to earn the life after death that he wished for. In addition, Jesus pointed out the attachment which held the young man back from achieving what he wanted; yet the young man could not break it. We read that when he heard the words of Jesus his 'face fell. He went away sad, because he had great wealth.' (Mark 10:21) In talking to his disciples about the young man, Jesus is clearly speaking about self-reliance when he says 'It is easier for a camel to go through the eye of a needle than for a rich man to enter the kingdom of God.' His followers, while understanding the hyperbole, are completely taken aback. After all, Jews believed that riches were a sign of God's blessing; if those who enjoyed God's blessing could not be saved, then who could be? The disciples ask 'Who then can be saved?' Jesus responds by saying that although it is impossible for humankind to be saved by self-reliance, salvation is possible with God's help. In other words, salvation is willingly given by God to rich and poor, good and bad alike. It is something which may only be received by those who are open; it may not be secured through self effort. This is difficult for Buddhists to accept as self-reliance appears morally responsible, while the opposite is viewed as irresponsible and, indeed, impossible. A Thai proverb says that the teacher cannot eat food for the student; the student needs to eat for himself in order to be well. A person may function as a teacher of the Christian way but that person cannot follow the way for the listener. The listener, if he is convinced of the 'rightness' of the Christian path, needs to decide *and* begin to follow Jesus Christ. I suppose making that decision and following through on it may reflect a lot of conflicting commitments and turmoil; and perhaps that could be referred to as self-effort? Insistence on self-reliance and the refusal to receive help from God will shut us off from knowing God. The rich young man who wanted to live with God in his kingdom in the age to come is a case in point.

But does liberation belong to the domain of humankind and does saving ourselves lie within our capability? A cat may chase a bird on the ground but the bird flies to the roof of a house. The cat would like to fly up and catch the bird, but flying is a capability the cat does not possess. The point here is that saving ourselves is beyond our ability. Trying to do what one is not created to do is folly, and the story of 'The Marsh Crow' from the *Jātaka* stories makes this point very well.[1] The Buddha tells the story of a marsh crow that caught fish in a pool; the marsh crow was joined by a land crow. The land crow admired the marsh crow catching fish and became the servant of the marsh crow. He would eat what was left of the marsh

---

[1] The *Jātaka* (contained in the *Khuddaka Nikāya*) are a collection of stories the Buddha told of 547 of his previous lives. Each story highlights a moral principle which helped him on his path to enlightenment. At the end of this story the Buddha indicated that he was the marsh crow while his jealous cousin, Devadatta, was the land crow.

crow's catch and take the rest to his mate. After a while the land crow became proud and thought he could catch his own fish. The marsh crow warned him that this was beyond his capabilities but the land crow refused to listen. The land crow tried to catch fish but got caught in the weeds and drowned. The marsh crow informed the mate of the land crow about the drowning and said:

> He was not born to dive beneath the wave,
> But what he could not do he needs must try;
> So the poor bird has found a watery grave,
> Entangled in the weeds, and left to die.

Fishing lay beyond the ability of the land crow, and saving or liberating ourselves lies beyond human capacity.

Initially, there appear to be similarities between the Buddhist and Christian paths. Rather than seeking refuge in the Buddha, *Dhamma* and *saṅgha*, a Christian will engage with God, the Christian Scriptures and the community of faith (church). The Buddhist does not depend on the Buddha like the Christian does on God: the Buddha is respected for discovering and passing on the *Dhamma* to others. In the Christian tradition, however, God is acknowledged as both the revealer of truth and the saviour of the world. Of course, those who are familiar with Buddhist practice will point out that many in Folk Buddhism will pray to the Buddha to do for them what they cannot do for themselves, and for them at least the Buddha is a saviour figure.

The writer's understanding of *karma*

Theologians have put forward a variety of understandings of the death of Christ: why it was necessary and what it achieved.

The writer's understanding of *karma*

These explanations have reflected the concerns of theologians and were conditioned by their historical and cultural contexts. Of course, we are also conditioned by our contexts and personal histories, but my question is how might the story of Jesus' death and resurrection best be explained to a Buddhist? Might we construct a redemptive analogy using the Buddhist understanding of *karma*?

Before we attempt this redemptive analogy I would like to put forward my own position on *karma*. With respect to those who believe in *karma*, I have to say that I do not find that it offers a convincing system of moral reward and punishment, given a being's lack of awareness of previous existences. For example, in this life a person may suffer oppression, separation from family, and perhaps even torture. A karmic explanation of this is that the person is reaping the negative karmic fruit from unskillful actions perhaps from previous lives. Yet if there is no recollection of previous lives and if the person is unable to relate the current set of difficult circumstances to actions in a previous life, (or lives) then to what extent is justice carried out? An effective form of retributive justice surely involves the culprit being made aware of the exact reason for the punishment. Indeed, the apparent disconnect between this and future lives may be a reason why some Buddhists are *not* motivated to do good in order to receive good in a future existence.

True, the Bible does talk about a person reaping what he sows. (e.g. Galatians 6:7) Clearly there is truth in that as a general principle, although we can probably give examples of when that did *not* seem to be true. On seeing a man who had been born blind the disciples asked Jesus if it was the man's sin or his parents' sin that he was born blind (John 9:2)—doesn't this sound a bit like moral cause and effect? Did the disciples believe that the blind man had a previous life in which he committed evil? The possibility of a child sinning in the womb was an issue discussed by the Jewish teachers (Beasley-Murray, 1999:155). No doubt they reflected on the struggle between Jacob and Esau in the womb of their mother Rebekah. (Genesis 25:19-26) In response, Jesus indicated that the blindness was not brought about by some pre-birth sin of the blind man, neither was it a punishment for some sin committed by the parents of the blind man. Jesus told his disciples that in this particular case the man's affliction, doubtless brought about by natural causes, was going to be used by him to demonstrate the power of God. (John 9:3) Most commentaries on this passage have interesting remarks about what happens when Jesus, the light of the world, shines in a dark place. I simply want to make the point that Jesus did not relate the massive disability of life-long blindness as being caused by a prior sin.

Buddhist understandings of *karma*

Karma and rebirth answer a number of questions for a Buddhist. For example, why do bad things happen to an apparently good person? One answer is that in a previous life the person led a good life—hence the comfortable current life—but committed a 'one off' intentionally bad crime and is now reaping the fruit of this unskillful karmic seed. *Karma* is a term that many non-Buddhists are familiar with, and, without understanding the details of the concept, generally agree with—*karma* ensures one gets what one deserves.

Karma (Sanskrit; Pali *kamma*) derives from a root meaning 'action' and means intended or volitional action. *Karma* may be considered as moral cause and effect and a natural law like the law of gravity, or the meteorological law that states that air moves from a high pressure area to a low pressure area.

The scholar monk Walpola Rahula states that 'if a good action produces good efforts and a bad action bad effects, this is not reward, or punishment, or justice. It is simply reproduction; the effect is in keeping with the cause.' If you plant a potato you will reap a potato, not a turnip. In Buddhist thought, there is no divine lawgiver or judge to reward or punish good or bad actions. Karmic laws of moral cause and effect carry out this function.

Traditional understandings of Buddhism teach that as a being passes away, it strives after another life and grasps at an emerging life form. The Buddha called craving a seamstress that sews together one life to another. Craving is incredibly powerful and produces a vast amount of suffering. On gaining insight into reality a person will cease to crave. The absence of craving means there is no 'engine' driving the being forward to rebirth, and consequently there is no 'next life'. Prior to the conception of a sentient being a union needs to take place between the sperm and the egg and the female must be at a fertile point in her cycle. In addition, a Buddhist believes that a karmic trace or stream of consciousness appropriate to the condition and status of this particular new life must be present before conception takes place.

We can separate *karma* into two categories. There is wholesome or skilful *karma*, or *kusala* (Pali), and its opposite, unwholesome or unskillful *karma*, called *akusula*, Wholesome *karma* is morally praiseworthy and spiritually helpful, and unwholesome *karma* is morally blameworthy and spiritually harmful. There are ten types of unwholesome *karma*, the first three are physical: taking life, taking what does not belong to you, and sexual misconduct. The next four are verbal: speaking falsehood, divisive speech, harsh speech, and engaging in idle chatter. The final three have to do with the mind. They are:

yearning for something that does not belong to you, having ill will toward someone else, and holding wrong views.

The ten types of wholesome *karma* are abstaining from the above and doing the opposite. We can distinguish between wholesome and unwholesome actions by asking ourselves if our intention is to do good or bad. If we take a course of action for the good of another person but it causes harm, then that is not an unwholesome action. A related question here is, what is our motivation in taking a particular course of action? Sometimes we may do a good thing for the wrong reason such as to manipulate a person; clearly this is not wholesome action.

A person is to a considerable extent shaped by their choices. A choice leaves an imprint in the mind which makes it easier to choose that particular course of action again. As one resists unwholesome desires, wise, compassionate characteristics develop. As the pattern of our actions are gradually changed, this results in a positive change of character. Of course, this is a slow process but gradually momentum is built up and the choices, either skillful or unskillful, become more natural. This was one reason why the Buddha emphasized being constantly mindful and used the illustration of a bucket being placed under a dripping pipe—after a while there is a bucket full of water. A person then is changed by his or her choices and this reminds us of the adage:

> Sow a thought and you will reap an act
> Sow an act and you reap a habit
> Sow a habit and you reap a character
> Sow a character and you reap a destiny.

As we know, a seed will ripen only if the soil, light and moisture conditions are appropriate. Similarly, a karmic action only matures when certain conditions are present. A clear, intentional action—skillful or unskillful—produces conducive conditions for the maturation of the *karma* seed. In terms of maturation there are three categories of *karma*. There is *karma* that will ripen in this lifetime; there is *karma* that will ripen in the next lifetime; and there is *karma* that will ripen at some point after that, perhaps many rebirths away. Karmic fruit, however, is not a reward or punishment; it is simply the outworking of the law of cause and effect in the moral realm.

We have already mentioned that *karma* determines rebirth and there are categories of *karma* which 'kick in' in order of priority as a being comes to the end of its life and is reborn. First, we have weighty or heavy *karma*; this is referred to as *garuka karma*. *Karma* of this nature has priority over other categories of *karma* and may be wholesome or unwholesome. The following 'causes' are considered to be heinous crimes which will very quickly produce negative 'effects': killing one's father or mother, murdering an enlightened one, wounding a Buddha, and creating a schism in the *saṅgha* (community of Buddhists, but often understood as the community of monks).

If there is no weighty *karma* which comes into effect, then the second category of *karma* 'kicks in'; this is referred to as death-proximate *karma*. If a good deed is done towards the end of a life and/or the final thoughts are ones of compassion and non-clinging, then rebirth will be positive. In fact, if a person about to be executed for murder shows genuine remorse for his crime and demonstrates a change of heart, he may be reborn in a good rebirth. He will, of course, have to suffer the full effect of his unskillful action. A good person who ends life by clinging to his existence, or thinks bitter thoughts may suffer a poor rebirth; however, in this poor rebirth he will experience the effect of the wholesome deeds he carried out.

Habitual *karma* is the third category. If there is no weighty *karma* and no significant death-proximate *karma*, then habitual *karma* comes into play. Indeed, this is what usually happens. This is the *karma* that is generated by constant repetition of thoughts, words and deeds, and is usually what causes rebirth.

Unpredictable or miscellaneous *karma* is the final category. This, as the name suggests, is unpredictable as to what will happen. Miscellaneous *karma* will come into play if all other forms of *karma* are not particularly dominant.

Buddhism sees a causal link between one life and another. We are a unified combination of five bundles, or *khanda*s, which are subject to arising and passing away; we are pulsations of matter coming together in material forms for a nanosecond. Each moment passes away and does not leave anything behind except an 'impression' or thought which is picked up by the next impression. The last impression of the dying being is transmitted across to the new life form. It then is the first impression of the new life and the stream of consciousness continues. This first impression contains a 'record' of every life previously lived associated with that stream of consciousness.

These categories of *karma* acting on a being that is passing over from one life to another are now diagrammed. The broken lines depicting the five components of being indicate interconnectedness to each other.

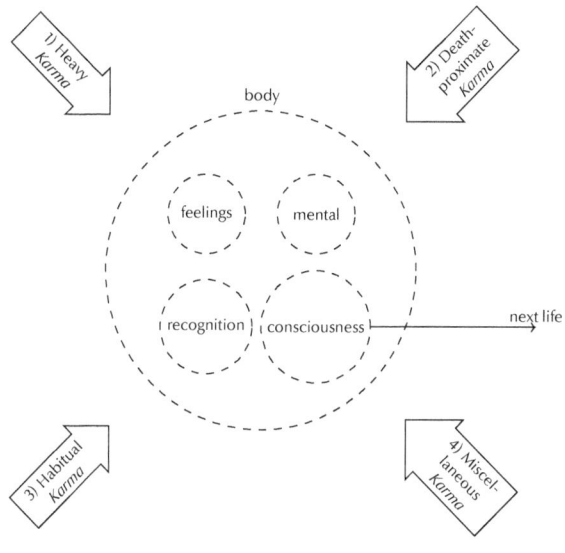

Rebirth as a human is comparatively rare and offers an excellent opportunity to achieve enlightenment. Human life, unlike that say of a *deva* in a heavenly plane, contains sufficient suffering to make us reflect on the reason for suffering. In addition, we have the potential for reasoning, meditating and engaging in meritorious deeds.

Those who die in a high level of meditation, where the mind is very calm and quiet, achieve rebirth into a heaven where existence is subtle and the mind is illuminated and at peace. This is still within the realms of *saṃsāra*, and so this existence is impermanent; death will take place, with consequential rebirth depending on the *karma* of the being. Death in a very high level of absorption will result in a birth in a formless heaven where existence is non-material, or 'mind-only'. This rebirth may last for up to 84,000 eons, but it is still impermanent.[2]

Most Buddhists believe that the situation people find themselves in is exactly what is deserved; it is simply reaping the results of past actions. Yet it would be wrong to view this as fatalistic—one may make wholesome choices, which can positively shape one's future. According to Buddhism, the aim of the *Dhamma* is to lead humankind to liberation; this reflects a moving beyond the laws of *karma*. By following the Eightfold Path at the higher level, the Buddhist focuses on what the Buddha called the *karma* that comes from keeping the Eightfold Path. This is referred to as the '*karma* that leads to enlightenment'. I am not defending the Buddhist core belief of *karma*, but perhaps we may use it to explain the Gospel to Buddhists.

A possible explanation of the death of Christ using the ideas of the 'middle man' and transfer of merit

A Buddhist reading the account of the crucifixion of Jesus may well conclude that this painful and shameful death was brought about by 'weighty *karma*' precipitated by some heinous crime. Of course, the long, excruciatingly painful process of crucifixion was designed to totally humiliate a victim as well as to highlight Roman supremacy. It functioned as a very powerful deterrent for anyone wishing to challenge the imperial rule of the Roman Empire. From a Buddhist perspective, the Jewish religious leaders and Roman authorities could have been mistaken in their assessment of Jesus, but for Buddhists, *karma* makes no mistakes. Yet according to Luke's

---

[2] The time it would take to wear down a seven mile high granite mountain by wiping it once a century with a piece of fine cloth is the time it takes for an eon (Sanskrit *kappa*) to pass. See Harvey (1990:33).

telling of this story, we find an astonishing demonstration of three key qualities much respected by Buddhists. These are: *mettā* (loving kindness), *karuṇā* (compassion) and *upekkhā* (even handedness). Here, in the context of unimaginable pain and public humiliation, Luke (23:34) comments that Jesus spoke to God and said 'Father, forgive them [those who played some part in the death of Christ], for they do not know what they are doing.' This is a remarkable insight into the character of the one who is being crucified.

A Christian explanation of the death of Jesus Christ may well draw on two ideas familiar to Asian Buddhists: the 'go-between' or middle person, and *punnadāna*, the transfer of merit. First, the middle person. If a person wishes to ask someone for a favour, rather than approaching the person directly he might ask a 'go-between' to ask on his behalf. This makes it easier for both parties. A 'go-between', however, needs to be acceptable to the person being petitioned as well as to the person who is petitioning. In this context, Christ, the Son of God, is acceptable to God because he is just as much God as God the Father and God the Holy Spirit. This may be seen from the following quote from a letter written shortly before 70 CE to converts from Judiasm to the 'Jesus Way'. In this letter Christ is depicted as a *great* High Priest who is now with God and different from other high priests of Judiasm who, of course, were not divine; who sometimes gave in to some of their temptations and were perhaps perceived by ordinary people as aloof.

> For we do not have a high priest who is unable to sympathize with our weaknesses, but we have one who has been tempted in every way, just as we are yet without sin. (Hebrews 5:15)

Christ is fully human and understands human limitations and vulnerabilities. Indeed, he was called the friend of sinners because he was often found talking, eating and drinking with people at the margins of society. 'Friend of sinners' was really a pejorative term used by the strict religious teachers of his time to suggest Jesus lacked moral discernment and was thus an inauthentic teacher. In Matthew 3:13-17 we have the story of Jesus offering himself for baptism. In this act he identifies with humankind. I can well imagine some of the Pharisees coming from Jerusalem to find out what was going on in terms of the many people who were being baptized by John the Baptist in the River Jordan. They probably would not have known the identity of Jesus but as they observed Jesus being baptized they may have wondered what sins he thought it necessary to turn away from. The practice of this kind of baptism was for people to indicate their turning to God and a looking forward to his coming kingdom. It would have been normal that once the baptism took place, people—for instance, soldiers and tax collectors—would ask John the Baptist for advice as how best to live (see Luke 3:12-14). Indeed, Matthew Henry (1995:18) points out that in Matthew 3:16, Christ, 'having no sins to confess, went up immediately out of the water' whereas others 'that were baptized stayed to confess their sins'. Not only does Jesus identify with humankind in this baptism story, God the Father identifies with Jesus the Son as the Spirit of God descends in the likeness of a dove. The identification is visual but also audible and a voice from heaven says 'This is my Son, whom I love: with him I am well pleased.'

Christ identifies with wrong-doers, yet he is fully God and connected to the other two persons of the Trinity: the Father and the Holy Spirit. Christ 'qualifies' as a middle man between both God and humankind. Indeed, it is for this purpose that he was born to a Jewish teenage girl.

The ideas of the 'middle man' and transfer of merit has long been used by Christians to explain the death of Christ to Buddhists. Jesus is both human and divine and in that sense may be compared to a 'middleman'. I think of the unskillful deeds I have done which, from a Buddhist perspective, is the sowing of bad karmic seed. As I read the Gospels, I see the skillful deeds of Christ. There are examples of compassionate acts of healing those who were physically and mentally ill, as well as befriending and affirming those from the margins of society such as a woman of dubious reputation and a tax collector—a member of a profession despised by Jews of that time. In addition, Christ taught complex concepts in everyday terms and challenged the religious leaders who had turned a covenant relationship with God into an excessively legalistic practice. Christ never, according to the Scriptures, carried out an unskillful action, and so from a Buddhist perspective, there would have been no negative karmic fruit to reap.

In contrast, we have all intentionally carried out 'unskillful deeds'. These actions have caused harm to others and have fallen short of our own personal standards, as well as those of our religious tradition. If there is no punishment for acts which have caused suffering to others then we live in an unfair world without hope of justice. Buddhists believe that *karma* ensures justice, while Christians believe that ultimately God will punish all wrong doing. Sometimes the Christian tradition is criticized because it talks about Hell. This is not the place to discuss the location, duration and temperature of such a place or state, but simply to point out that Buddhism also has its hells. Indeed, the breaking of the Buddhist precepts[3] will

---

[3] The Five Precepts are basic standards which Buddhists try to maintain. They may be viewed as training rules to help a person develop. These are: No taking of life, no taking of what is not given, no illicit sex, no speaking of falsehoods and no use of mind-altering substances.

result in rebirth in one of these hells.[4] There is a belief that the hell we end up in is appropriate to our wrong doing. The duration of time in one of these hells may be measured in vast periods of time but it is not permanent, and ultimately there will be a more pleasant rebirth.

To continue with this redemptive analogy for the Buddhist context, we may say that when Jesus Christ died on the cross he suffered the negative results of all wrongdoing. In Buddhist terms, we have all sowed negative karmic seed, but Christ reaps the negative karmic fruit from these unskilful actions. Until we acknowledge that we have done wrong and that Christ functioned both as a substitute and as a hero on our behalf to liberate us, we remain connected to our negative karmic actions and their consequences. This acknowledgement of having behaved unskilfully and the acceptance of the reality that Christ does for us what we are unable to do for ourselves requires a significant mental shift for non-Christians.

We may think here of the family of a layman who ordains as a Buddhist monk. A huge amount of merit is gained by the family through that sacrificial and perhaps financially costly act. We may look at the event through the eyes of a mother who clearly is unable to ordain as a monk herself. The mother approvingly gives up her son to the monkhood and, as a result, participates in the benefits of his meritorious action. This approval is seen as she places her hands together in the traditional posture of respect and, most likely but not necessarily, saying 'it is good', or 'well done'. This is an example of the

---

[4] Some Buddhists do not view these as literal realms, saying that they are Hindu constructs while the Buddha taught that heaven and hell are in the 'here and now'. This is typified by the well-used Thai proverb, 'Heaven is in your chest while hell is in your heart.'

Buddhist virtue of *mutidā*, or rejoicing in the joy of others.[5] If for some reason the mother were *not* to approve of the son's ordination then she would not participate in the merit which allegedly accrues from this action. One reason for this might be that the mother is not a Buddhist and has serious misgivings about her son's action; or it may be that she is a Buddhist but wishes her son to remain at home with her, rather than going away to become a Buddhist monk.

In a similar way we can choose to rejoice in the meritorious action of Christ on our behalf, or not. If we do not believe in his action, it would naturally be disingenuous of us to accept it. Or it may well be that we think it is true, but do not wish to make a commitment. It may be very different from what our family and friends believe and we do not wish to alienate them. And, of course, it is very hard to admit to having behaved unskillfully. To conclude this redemptive analogy using Buddhist terms: in accepting Christ as our middleman between us and God, not only is the karmic bond to our sin broken, the good *karma* generated by Christ's skillful actions becomes ours. A new karmic link is formed and the story of this 'middleman' becomes our story. Not to voice our approval or acceptance of what Christ has done means we do not receive the benefits he offers us.

A Buddhist response to the use of *karma* to explain the Christian understanding of the death of Christ

Some Buddhists, mainly within the Theravāda tradition, argue that a transfer of merit cannot take place except in the case of

---

[5] We already mentioned the virtues of *mettā*, *karuṇā* and *upekkhā* in connection with Christ's attitude towards those responsible for his crucifixion. *Mutidā* completes the group of four highly valued qualities.

a human to a departed relative who has become a ghost (*peta* Pali). Of course, the ghost needs respite in the hellish existence it is experiencing. The Buddha told King Bimbisara a story to express his appreciation for a meal which the king provided. At the end of the story (known as 'Outside the Walls')[6] some Brahmins asked 'Do our relatives who have become ghosts benefit from our donations carried out in their name?' The Buddha responded by saying that any merit made would be of no merit to a relative who has been reborn in a hell, or as an animal, human, or heavenly being. The relative, however, who is reborn as a ghost (*peta*) does receive the benefit generated by the offerings of family and friends. The Brahmins wanted to know if they made an offering with the wish that the merit be transferred to a relative and that particular relative was not in the realm of the ghosts, then who would receive the benefit of the offering. The Buddha responded that the ghosts would receive the offering and all of us were bound to have some relatives who were ghosts and so the merit would benefit these relatives.

Based on these teachings of the Buddha we learn that the merit of a good deed will benefit those who have been reborn as *petas* but not those in other realms. The *peta* may be considered as homeless, stateless, without the capacity for fending for itself, and so depends on the generosity of human relatives. We also learn that the donation to the monks carried out by the relative brings some benefit to the relative. In the words of the Buddha, 'those who donate an offering are not without fruit.' All of the merit goes to the ghost, but the donor is left with the pleasure of having discharged his duty and having overcome the inclination to keep rather than give.

---

[6] The *Peta* Stories or are found in the *Khuddaka Nikāya* in the *Sutta Piṭṭaka*

It is generally accepted that the transfer of merit from humans to departed relatives who exist in the ghost realm is part of the teachings of the Buddha. This idea corresponds to our psychological need to do something for our departed loved ones. The ghost has been taken beyond self-reliance, crying out for help in his dismal existence and expressing gratitude when he receives it. Buddhism has a very high view of the human condition, seeing it as a great opportunity for making merit, unlike the condition of a ghost. But how much merit is 'enough merit' and how do we know? Perhaps we are more like the ghosts than we think!

Some Theravādin Buddhists who take a more theoretical approach to their tradition may further object to our *karma* analogy by pointing out that an enlightened being has moved beyond *karma* and therefore does not have *karma* to share with others. This is reflected in the saying, 'Just as a bird flies across the sky without a trace, so the enlightened being moves through life leaving no karmic trace.' They would not deny that an enlightened being brings benefit to all who come in contact with him, but would not see how one who has moved beyond merit could transfer merit to those who look to him for it.

Some years ago, I was trying to resolve the issue of the concept of a transfer of merit in Theravāda Buddhism and I emailed my question to the abbot of a Buddhist monastery. Here is his reply:

> Greetings Rory,
>
> Sorry for the delay in replying.
>
> I fear I am not the best person to ask such speculative questions. I never ponder on such matters. In fact it might well be the case that the Buddha also

would discourage such speculation. But in case he wouldn't then I would say that almost certainly 'someone else benefits from the skilful deeds of an *arahat*'. Skilful deeds always lead to well-being. But basically the question rests on the assumption of there being an individual self, which for an *arahat* is obviously a non-issue. And the whole question of making merit is only an issue for those who are concerned about such things. An *arahat* is obviously not. As to whether or not an *arahat* makes merit, I believe there have been arguments about this from way back, and there appears to be statements supporting both sides including in the Scriptures, but please don't ask me where to find them. But why are you interested in this anyway? I would like to hear.

Meanwhile, best wishes and looking forward to meeting your students,

Ajahn M

The *bodhisattva* ideal, an essential feature of Mahāyāna Buddhism, means that an enlightened being will carry out actions which lead to the benefit and ultimate liberation of others. Indeed, the motivation of the *bodhisattva* to become enlightened is to facilitate the liberation of all sentient beings. We must not, however, isolate the *bodhisattva* to Mahayanna Buddhism; it is certainly present in more folk orientated expressions of Theravāda Buddhism, as we shall see in the Appendix.

Mahāyāna Buddhism and the transfer of merit

Since we are experiencing resistance from some theoretical Theravāda Buddhists to the *karma* analogy to explain the benefits of Christ's death, let us move on to the Mahāyāna tradition! This idea of someone doing for you what you cannot do for yourself is more readily accepted within some of the Mahāyāna traditions; I am thinking here in particular of Pure Land Buddhism. In this tradition, Gotama, the Historical Buddha, told his attendant Ānanda the story of Dharmākara, who in many eons previously vowed before a Buddha that he would create a perfect land for all who suffer. The Buddha went on to explain that the *bodhisattva* Dharmākara went on to become the Buddha of Infinite Light (Amida / Amitāba) and created a paradise or Pure Land in the West referred to as Sukhāvatī. Shinran (1173-1262), a famous master in the Japanese Pure Land tradition, taught that humankind had become too corrupt to save itself and that liberation could only come from trusting in Amitāba. In this tradition there is a strong focus on 'other power'—the power of the Amitāba Buddha—rather than 'self power'. Shinran taught that:

> [E]ven a single act of faith in Amida [Amitāba] was sufficient; repeating his name on subsequent occasions earned no extra merit but was merely a way of expressing thanks to Amida. Even faith would be a temptation to pride for some people and Shinran stressed that faith in Amida is a gift from Amida and not something we achieve for ourselves. (Cush, 1994:58)

Shinran certainly moved away from the teaching of his master Hōnen (1133-1212) who placed a very strong emphasis on a complete trust in the Amitiba Buddha and a repeating of his name with intense belief. The Pure Land rebirth was not something then that was earned—a reward for an intense and sustained faith—but a gift from a merciful enlightened being. Little wonder that when the Jesuits reached Japan in the 16th century they confused Pure Land Buddhism with Protestant Christianity and initially lamented that Martin Luther had arrived in Japan before them! Pure Land's emphasis on salvation through grace drew fire from other Buddhists who sometimes accused them of neglecting Buddhist moral teaching and effort.[7]

Of course, gratitude for Amitāba's gift of unconditional salvation could lead a Pure Land Buddhist to moral excellence, performing acts of kindness out of gratitude, and having a lifestyle of gratitude and service which contributes to the liberation of all beings. I was intrigued to discover recently that a Pure Land Buddhist compared the nature of the Pure Land to the Kingdom of God.[8] There is a similarity between this understanding of Pure Land Buddhism and Christianity. Christians understand that they currently live in the Kingdom of God and that, through prayer, witness and deeds of service, they contribute to the advance of God's Kingdom and the restoration of all things to their original purpose. Christians are saved not simply to be 'safe' but to serve others in Christ's name, and God's presence gives the capacity to live 'for the kingdom'.

---

[7] There is a helpful introduction to Pure Land Buddhism in Cush, 1994:155-160.

[8] In an interview with Jim Pym, Edinburgh, 24th January 2014. Mr Pym is a Pure Land Buddhist, scholar and mystic.

> A Buddhist monk saw an elderly lady walking past on the way to her Pure Land temple and he called out:
>
> 'Well, Granny, on your way to the Pure Land?'
>
> The woman smiled and nodded.
>
> 'I expect Amida is there waiting for you,' said the monk
>
> The woman shook her head violently, looking puzzled.
>
> 'If he's not in the Pure Land then where is he?' the monk asked.
>
> The woman looked at him pityingly, tapped her heart three times and went on her way.
>
> The monk admitted defeat, saying, 'There goes a true Pure Land devotee.' (Pym, 2001:104)

The story illustrates Pym's (2001:100) point that the Pure Land is:

> [A] place in which we can be reborn after our present life is over, and also a state of being in the here and now. Birth in the Pure Land is the result of Amida's vow, and we can accept it at any time. It is not necessary for us to die before we can personally experience that power.

Another significant point of contact between Pure Land Buddhism and Christianity is the way in which followers of both traditions look beyond self effort for salvation. Pym (2001:103) comments:

> [T]here is no need for us to 'do' anything to bring about our birth in the Pure Land. Instead, we need to 'undo'; to let go of all our self-power and efforts to become enlightened, as they get us nowhere. As we let go of our own efforts, we are grasped by the Light of Amida's Compassion, and our birth in the Pure Land is assured. This state is called *Shinjin*.

Pure Land Buddhists not only place a trust in something beyond themselves—Amida—they believe that Amida takes care of the *karma* generated by their unskillful actions. Two comments from Professor Inagaki illustrate this: 'When we encounter Amida's Pure Light, all our karmic bonds and impurities are removed, leaving in us pure and serene entrusting hearts.' (Inagaki, 2000:14) Also, 'Amida's Light of Pure Wisdom is bound to penetrate to the depths of our existence and dissolve our tenacious bonds. With our impure *karma* cancelled by Amida's pure *karma*, we enjoy participation in his pure activity, expressing our gratitude by the *Nembutsu* ["I take refuge in the name of Amida Buddha"].' (Inagaki, 2000:18)

Karma is viewed by Buddhists as an irrevocable law of the cosmos and somehow ensures that justice is done. While there is no god in Buddhism upholding the function of intentional action and consequent effect, from a Buddhist perspective *karma* ensures that there is an effect to the intentional cause. Christians believe that God ensures that sin is punished and, for that matter, that good actions are rewarded. If this were not the case, then the moral government of the universe would be compromised and justice would not take place. This ensuring of ultimate justice for everyone both highlights the gravity of sin (unskillful action) and the fairness of God.

The unembracable are embraced at the cross: three paradoxes of the death of Christ

We have discussed the death of Christ in regard to the 'middle man' and the transfer—or, more accurately, the exchanging—of merit, both good and bad. We may respond positively or otherwise to this redemptive analogy but of key importance is the sharing of the story of the death and resurrection of Jesus with our Buddhist friends. To do this is to partner with God in his mission in the world, and to know his empowering presence. As we affirm the centrality and transforming power of the cross let us consider three paradoxes we see there. These are: beauty in disfigurement, omnipotence in weakness, and togetherness in separation.

While sinful acts cause damage in the community in which they are committed, they also contradict, even strike at, the moral goodness of God. This violation of God's moral goodness needs to be dealt with as it separates us from God. Japanese theologian and pastor Kazoh Kitamori (1916-1998) points out something of the suffering of God, not only in the human violation of his holy standards, but also in the process of winning back a wayward humanity. Kitamori (1965:22) movingly writes:

> The Lord was unable to resolve our death without putting himself to death. God himself was broken, was wounded, and suffered, because he embraced those who should not be embraced. By embracing our reality, God grants us absolute peace.

Christ, at the point of his death, cries out 'My God, my God why have you forsaken me?' (Matthew 27:46) Here, in the mystery of Christ's suffering, we encounter three significant paradoxes. In the first we see that the divine Son has been beaten up so brutally that he is not recognizable as Jesus from Nazareth. (Isaiah 52:14) And yet, for the Christian believer, Christ is at his loveliest, despite his marred physical appearance.

In the second paradox, the Son appears to have been completely subjugated by Roman power and law—and yet he is in the process of triumphing over all powers, seen and unseen. The Jews would have looked at the Son of God on the tree of shame and seen a person cursed by God and ritually impure, yet the text indicates that as a result of his sacrifice the Son will sprinkle many nations. (Isaiah 52:15) That is to say, he will conduct a priestly act of purification for the people of these many nations. The *events* of the cross were located in Jerusalem yet the *effects* spread throughout the cosmos.

The third paradox is separation and togetherness. As all sin, past, present and future is drawn to the cross through some centripetal spiritual force, it is little wonder that there is an apparent disruption of the Father and his Son, for sin divides, separates and breaks up all kinds of relationships. Yet the underlying reality of the Father being One with the Son (John 17:21-22) is demonstrated in their unity of purpose to see a way made possible for humankind to be reconciled to God.

So the final words of Christ are recorded for us in Luke 23:44, where we read, 'Jesus called out with a loud voice "Father, into your hands I commit my spirit." When he said this, he breathed his last.' The point that many commentators have made from this verse is that the Son voluntary gives up his spirit when he chooses to, as opposed to being executed by the crucifixion process.

My purpose, however, in mentioning the verse "Father, into your hands I commit my spirit" is to note that if there was an element of abandonment of the Son by the Father it was for a brief moment. Some Bible commentators have expressed the view that the Father is repulsed by the sin which Christ bore. (see 2 Corinthians 5:21; Galatians 3:13) Others tend to view the godforsaken experience of Jesus as the inability of the Father to look on his suffering Son who sacrifices himself in the power of the Holy Spirit. Both of these positions indicate how the one was affected by the other, and give us a picture of a Father who has momentarily lost his Son because of sin, or suffering, and a Son who has lost sight of his Father. Possibly Moltmann (1974:243) is correct to comment:

> Thus the delivering up of the Son to godforsakenness is the ground for the justification of the godless and the acceptance of enmity by God. It may therefore be said that the Father delivers up his Son on the cross in order to be the Father of those who are delivered up.

From a substitution perspective, redemption and reconciliation to God turn on these godforsaken moments on the cross. Certainly there is hope in this image for all those who experience abandonment in its many different forms. Also, in a similar way, there is much here to inform our understanding of the nature of suffering. Bauckham (1995:63), however, reminds us when theologizing about the suffering of God to 'distinguish between what can be said of God *as human* (in the incarnation) and what can be said of him *as God* (outside incarnation).' Indeed he goes on to caution:

> God suffers, but as the one who transcends all finite suffering. We may say that there is something analogous to human suffering in the divine

> experience, but that we may not therefore claim that we know what it is like for God to suffer. (Bauckham, 1995:69)

Part then of God embracing us, the 'unembraceable', is the punishing of our sins; this involves the Father, Son and Spirit in a suffering beyond human imagination. The cross, often viewed as a lightening conductor for the anger of God, should also remind us of what sin does to God and why the suffering of its penalty is the only way that relationships between God and humankind can be restored. It is not only God's righteous anger with sin that is turned away because of Christ's death, the pain of God is relieved as he embraces prodigal daughters and sons for the first time since Adam's rebellion.

But is it not the case that some forms of substitution are acceptable while others are not? I often find myself paying for my daughter's parking fines, because that is not something she will make the time to do. I cannot, however, accept penalty points on my driving license for a speeding offence committed by my daughter. Is it permissible, then, for God the Father to place the wrongdoings of others on his innocent son, Jesus Christ, who then vicariously suffers the guilt, shame and penalties due to these wrong actions as if they were his? To put it mildly, this cuts across what we humans consider to be fair. Louis Berkhof (1971:379) reminds us that it was not God the Father who placed wrongdoing on Jesus Christ, God the Son. It was God—Father, Son and Holy Spirit—who conceived and agreed this vicarious suffering for the penalty of human wrong doing. God the Son and God the Holy Spirit were just as violated as God the Father by human wrongdoing. Although Christ's suffering is much more visible than that of the two other persons of the Trinity, is not necessarily greater. Through the pain and suffering of the cross and all its complex dimensions come great gain for humanity, and greater glory for God, as people are reconciled to Him, and all of creation returned to its original glory.

When Adam sinned, he sinned as the representative of all of humanity and so all of humanity—indeed, all sentient life—suffers the consequences of his action. Adam had the capacity to resist or succumb to the temptation of Satan to defy God's law and eat of the fruit of the Tree of the Knowledge of Good and Evil. (Genesis 2:17) The real possibility of disobeying God meant both freedom and responsibility for the first humans, and obeying God was a voluntary act of worship for Adam and Eve. Had they continued to follow God's instruction, they would have developed in their knowledge of and friendship with God. In time, they may have reached a stage where they and their descendents would not die but live forever. Sin, suffering and death enter the human experience as a consequence of Adam's rebellion against God. This fracturing of the human-divine friendship has significant implications for us all, as Adam was functioning as the representative of humanity. Paul writes 'For just as though the disobedience of the one man [Adam] the many were made sinners [all of us], so also through the obedience of the one man [Jesus Christ] the many [those who accept God's offer of forgiveness] will be made righteous. (Romans 5:19)

I appreciate that the concept of representation which we have just mentioned may appear unfair to some—it speaks of suffering the consequences of someone else's actions. Yet we all recognize that decisions made by our representatives have implications for us all; be they our leaders at our work, politicians, or an army in the case of a country at war.

Conclusion

This chapter has examined Buddhist understandings of *karma*. We have seen how *karma* functions at the point of passing over from one life to the next and how *karma* determines the realm in which rebirth takes place. The role of the intermediary was used to explain Christ's reconciling role between God and humankind. We explored the concept of the transfer of merit and suggested a redemptive analogy where Christ reaps all the negative karmic fruit which will grow as a consequence of all the intentional unskilful actions carried out by humankind. Some resistance to this redemptive analogy was identified among some Theravāda Buddhists who were not sympathetic to folk understandings of Buddhism. From a Buddhist perspective, hungry ghosts are considered to be incredibly weak and require an injection of merit in order to move them on from the realm they occupy. This is not the case for the beings in the other realms, as they must reap the negative fruit of their intentional actions. Humans are able to carry out meritorious deeds which may be transferred to a departed relative who is now suffering as a hungry ghost but not to any other being.

Mahāyāna Buddhism, with its strong emphasis on the concept of the *bodhisattva*, responds more positively to our transfer-of-merit analogy. This analogy is similar to the idea of 'God equals *Dhamma*'; they are both imperfect models, but they may assist Buddhists to move towards a deeper understanding of the Christian path. The next chapter looks at another perspective on the death of Christ: his conquering of dark forces.

Pause for reflection

1. What is your view of using the concepts of *karma* and the transfer of merit to communicate the gospel? What

might someone who disagreed with your view say? How would you respond to that person?

2. Some theologians argue that God is immune to suffering as suffering implies change, and God is unchanging. They would also argue that the bliss and blessed state of God should not be impaired by the sins and suffering of human kind. There is an assumption then that suffering is wrong. Do you think that the concept of a God who is beyond suffering is more readily accepted by a Buddhist than a God who suffers? Is that different from your understanding of God?

Chapter 7

Christ's Triumph Over Dark Forces And The End Of Suffering

This final chapter briefly engages with Christ's triumph over dark forces and his work of bringing back this broken world to its original state of peace without suffering. It is fair to say that involvement with the spirit world is a normal part of life for many Asian Buddhists. Promises are made to spirits and pacts are entered into which prove to be unhealthy, even damaging. There is a need for people to be delivered from damaging relationships, but finding a way out is often difficult. This book has not discussed this important but sometimes complex aspect of mission; however, it raises the issue of Christ's triumph over dark forces. These dark forces will ultimately be destroyed, but people can be set free from their influence now. The other aspect of the title—'the end of suffering'—is surely relevant to Buddhists. After all, the Buddha dedicated his life to discovering the cause of and solution to suffering, and then teaching others what he had discovered.

We now move on to another way of understanding Christ's work on the cross, and the material is organized under the heading of two trees both of which are found in the Bible. The first tree, the Tree of Shame, is where Christ triumphed over dark forces. The second, the Tree of Life, is a breath-taking symbol of all things being made new by Christ. In terms of time, 2000 years have passed since the events of the first tree, and we have not reached the second tree where all things will be reconciled to their original purpose. Yet this is an exciting era to be living in; and it is a time for prayerful action. As we involve ourselves in God's mission, we believe that God will take our weak efforts and use them in some small way to the achieving of His purposes. This participation with God and others brings about considerable growth in many different areas of our lives.

The Tree of Shame and Christ's Triumph

The idea of referring to the cross on which Christ was crucified as a 'tree' comes from a verse in 1 Peter 2:24: 'He himself bore our sins in his body on the tree, so that we might die to sins and live for righteousness.' The word 'tree' (literally 'wood') is a euphemism for the cross, for there is a deep sense of shame and humiliation associated with crucifixion. During a holiday in Portugal, I visited the house of a prominent Roman Catholic family, which now functions as a museum. I was surprised that there were no crucifixes in the public rooms. The tour guide informed me that crucifixes were not displayed in public rooms out of respect for the many non-Roman Catholics who visited the house and would have been taken aback at such a symbol of torture. Indeed, she went on to say that her tour company had a policy of not allowing its guides to wear crucifixes or crosses which were visible as the sight of these may shock those from other religious traditions. She concluded, 'What is nice for us may not be nice for others.'

On the Tree of Shame, a cosmic victory of huge significance was won through the sin-bearing death of Christ. The crucifixion of Christ must have appeared to be the death of a criminal to the vast majority of bystanders, yet there are a number of supernatural activities which indicate that there was something other going on than simply a slow and painful execution. These supernatural signs include an earthquake, the splitting of rocks, and the emerging from the dead of many righteous people who went to Jerusalem and appeared to a good number of people. (Matthew 27:51-53) The release of these righteous people from death and their appearance in Jerusalem may well have happened on Easter Sunday and is symbolic of the way in which all people will come alive out of their state of death. The hardened Roman executioners were terrified as a result of the earthquakes, splitting rocks and darkness, and exclaimed 'Surely he [Jesus] was the Son of God'. (Matthew 27:54)

Christ suffered the effects of our sinful deeds—or to put it in Buddhist terms, reaped the bad karmic fruit which grew as a result of the negative karmic seed which has been sown. We read that:

> God forgave us all our sins having cancelled the written code, with its regulations, that was against us and that stood opposed to us; he took it away, nailing it to the cross. (Colossians 2:13-14)

Indeed, Martin (1974:84) reminds us that there 'is evidence, drawn from the Old Testament and Jewish literature to show that the idea of a book of works kept by God and recording all men's sins was familiar.'

In the previous chapter we compared the substitution understanding of the death of Christ with the concept of the transfer of merit. The model we use in this chapter has a different emphasis, and focuses on the victory of Christ over sinister forces through his death and resurrection. The *Christus Victor* (Christ the Victor) understanding of the atonement is a view which was has been brought to our attention through the writings of Swedish theologian Gustav Aulen (1879–1977) in his book *Christus Victor*, published in English in 1931. Theologians who prioritize this model of the atonement believe it to have been the dominant view of the Church in the first 1000 years of its existence. The Christus Victor position posits that Satan pressed God to enforce the penalty of the law on all who broke it.[1] Thus, in Buddhist terms, a record of all human 'unskilful karmic action' is placed on the cross. Christ signs this record as if these actions were his and this was his personal 'IOU', his own certificate of debt to God. This legal document is placed in a public place and Christ suffers the effects of these actions as he dies under the penalty due to the list of sins. It

---

[1] In chapter nine of his *The Cross of Christ* (1986), John Stott talks about the six stages of the conquest of Christ over evil and, in the process, provides us with a good overview of the *Christus Victor* model of the atonement. These are: 1. God predicts that Satan will be defeated by Christ; 2. Jesus overcomes Satan throughout his ministry. The most obvious example of this was his refusal to give in to the devil's temptations during his 40 day fast in the wilderness; 3. Jesus conquers the devil as he gives up his life voluntarily on the cross; 4. The resurrection of Christ from the dead is a confirmation of Christ's triumph over all dark powers; 5. Christ's conquest is extended as the Church goes out in mission to tell of Christ's triumph over evil and invite people to turn to God; 6. We look forward to the conquest of Christ over all evil powers at his return to this earth. At this point death will be destroyed and all things returned to their original pristine state.

is little wonder that the Son feels forsaken by his Father, for how could the Father look upon the agony of his only Son, innocent but overshadowed with the sins of the world? In this process, all record of sin is wiped out and the image is that of the expunging of any writing on a piece of papyrus. Any accusation made by the devil or other demonic forces against those who rely on this act of Christ for forgiveness of sins has no legal basis. The loving-kindness of Christ, and indeed the Father, prove to be stronger than all the dark forces; thus we read 'And [Christ] having disarmed the powers and authorities, he made a public spectacle of them, triumphing over them by the cross.' (Colossians 2:15)

The main emphasis of the Christus Victor understanding is Christ's defeat over the dark forces who are in revolt against God. These dark forces were once angelic beings created to serve God and, while invested with considerable power, chose to revolt against God's cosmic supremacy. Certainly as we read through the Gospel accounts, we notice that Christ is in conflict with dark powers as he exorcises evil spirits and heals people. Indeed, when 72 of Christ's disciples returned from a ministry trip they enthusiastically informed Jesus that the demons submitted to them when they used his authority. Jesus responded that he 'saw Satan fall like lightning from heaven'. (Luke 10:18)

Sometimes the devil is referred to as the 'prince of this world'; we will briefly examine a cluster of three instances of the use of this title toward the end of Christ's life on earth. First, at the Feast of the Passover, Christ indicates that 'now is the time for judgment on this world: now the prince of this world will be driven out'. (John 12:31) This could well be judgment on the world over which the devil has control. Leon Morris (1984:531) suggests that Satan has the title 'prince of this world' because he is the ruler of the human mind and certainly what is in evidence here is deceitful and deluded thinking on the part of threatened and jealous Jewish religious leaders. Calvin (1959:42) takes the view that this judgment is a re-ordering, or a restoring of this world. This certainly fits in with the idea that 'God did not send his son into the world to condemn the world but to save the world through him [Christ].' (John 3:17) Indeed, we may connect this with Paul's statement in Colossians, 1:19-20:

> For God was pleased to have all his fullness dwell in him [Christ], and through him to reconcile to himself all things, whether things on earth or things in heaven by making peace through his blood, shed on the cross.

Second, after the Passover meal and shortly before his trial, Christ says to his disciples, 'I will not speak with you much longer, for the prince of this world is coming. He has no hold on me.' (John 14:30) The prince of this world is coming in the sense that he is particularly active in his influence over Judas and the religious leaders who have been intent on bringing about Christ's death. Christ states that, despite prolonged and intense demonic opposition, the devil has 'nothing on him' because he has not carried out any unskilful action.

Third, and just before Christ leaves the house where he celebrated the Feast of the Passover with his disciples, he talks about the coming of the Holy Spirit and what He would do when He came. This appears to suggest that the Spirit would work in the lives of those who do not follow Christ, to make them aware of their inappropriate behaviour which is unacceptable to God and indeed others. Presumably the Spirit's influence would normally be through the Christian Scriptures and those who speak from them. In addition, people testify to dreams and visions where they have encountered God. At the end of this section Christ comments that 'the prince of the world now stands condemned'. (John 16:8-11) This prince (Satan) is the chief rebel against God and a leader of those who oppose the existence of the Kingdom of God. There is, therefore, an unmasking and humiliation of the prince of this world through the events of the death and resurrection of Christ, and not only him but all those who are in revolt against God.

John understands 'that the whole world is under the control of the evil one'. (1 John 5:19) Paul describes Satan as the 'ruler of the kingdom of the air, the spirit who is now at work in those who are disobedient'. (Ephesians 2:2) Paul is writing to new followers of Christ many of whom had come out of an occult background. Toward the end of his letter, he compares the Christian life to a wrestling match, not against other humans but against spiritual forces hostile towards God. His imagery of wrestling would not have been lost on those familiar with the 'winner takes all' wrestling competitions which took place in Ephesus, present-day Turkey. Paul writes:

> For our struggle is not against flesh and blood, but against the rulers, against the powers of this dark world and against the spiritual forces of evil in the heavenly realms. (Ephesians 6:12)

Paul goes on to compares the use of spiritual disciplines such as praying, reading and reflecting on Scripture, faith in God and so on, to parts of a Roman soldier's armour—a familiar sight in Ephesus at that time.

Another concept we could use to explain what Christ did on behalf of all those who trust in him is that of the hero who acts on behalf of others. The story is told of Queen Srisuriyothai who in 1549, disguised herself as a man, mounted an elephant and went out to observe a battle between the invading Burmese army and the Siamese. At one point her husband, King Chakkraphat, was in danger of losing his life, and if he were killed it would mean the fall of the capital Ayutthaya and the capturing of Siam by the invading Burmese army.[2] Queen Srisuriyothai drove her elephant between her husband's elephant and that of the Burmese king; this action is said to have saved her husband from death and her country from defeat. In the process she lost her own life.[3] Perhaps we could cast Christ in the role of a military hero like Queen Srisuriyothai, who died a violent death in order to ensure an entire nation remained free.

The Christian story does not end with a dead hero, but with a conqueror who came back to life. The concept of Christ as a conqueror is a widely held view within the Christian faith. The main emphasis of this idea is Christ vanquishing the dark forces which are in revolt against God. This created a situation of spiritual warfare between good and evil forces. We catch glimpses of this in the Gospels where the devil tries to cause Christ to sin during a 40 day period in the wilderness.[4] In this private power encounter, however, Christ demonstrates his

[2] Prince Thianracha was the uncle of Prince Yot Fa and on the appointment of his nephew to the throne became a Buddhist monk in order to avoid the volatile political situation. In 1548 he was recalled from the monastery and became King of Ayudhya. He took the name Chakkaphat meaning the 'wheel-turning, universal monarch, a king whose righteousness and might makes all the world revolve around him'. (D. Wyatt, 1984:91)

[3] See John R Davis (1998). *Poles Apart?: Contextualizing the Gospel in Asia.* Bangalore, India: Theological Book Trust:70. The Thai word for heroine is *wira saatrii*.

[4] There are some parallels between Satan tempting Christ and Māra trying to hold the Buddha back from enlightenment.

superior power. A giving-in to any of the devil's subtle temptations would have resulted in a loss of Christ's sinless status, resulting in the failure of his mission to liberate humankind from the control of demonic power.

The writer of the letter to Hebrew Christians argues that the death of Christ destroys the devil who holds the power of death and sets free those who are afraid of death (Hebrews 2:14-15). This theme of destruction is picked up by a later New Testament writer, who explains the purpose of Christ's coming into the world: 'The reason the Son of God appeared was to destroy the devil's work.' (1 John 3:8)

Three days after Christ's death he rose from the dead.[5] Neither the military expertise of Rome nor the sinister unseen forces we know so little about could prevent Christ's resurrection. This is viewed by Christians as a demonstration of his power over death, and over the dark forces which both harassed him during his time on earth and influenced the Jewish leaders to push for his execution. It is a proclamation to humanity and to the unseen world of cosmic beings that Christ is a conqueror.

The Tree of Life and the End of Suffering

We now come to the Tree of Life which stands on each side of the water of life which flows down the middle of the great street of the city, the New Jerusalem. This tree which constantly bears fruit has leaves for the healing of the nations. (Revelation 22:1-5) We first read of the Tree of Life at the beginning of the Bible. (Genesis 2:9) Had Adam and Eve eventually

---

[5] It should not be hard for a Buddhist who accepts the concept of rebirth to believe in the resurrection. The followers of Jesus would have expected him to rise from the dead one day, but not three days, after his crucifixion.

eaten from the fruit of that tree, and not from the Tree of the Knowledge of Good and Evil, they and their descendants may have never died. As a result of fracturing their relationship with their creator, Adam and Eve are denied access to the Tree of Life by a cherubim and flaming sword. (Genesis 3:24) This may be seen as an act of kindness by God—'a severe mercy' to use a phrase from CS Lewis. J. Wyatt (2009:71) comments:

> In God's providential care of his creation, then, human beings are not meant to live for ever in their degraded fallen state. The human lifespan is limited, not just as a curse, but out of God's grace. The flaming sword reminds us that human ingenuity and power cannot force a route to the tree of life.

The idea of the Tree of Life is one of peace without suffering, a quality of life which will neither diminish nor end. The tree, of course, is not the source of this peaceful life uninterrupted by death, but a symbol of God's life-giving presence. It points to the return of Jesus Christ, the cosmic conqueror, to this world and to the earth on which he walked after his resurrection from the dead. At this point, all powers and people will acknowledge the supremacy of Christ and it is here that all rebellion will be terminated, all remaining evil forces will be destroyed, and death will be no more. This is the point toward which all of history is moving, when Christ will reconcile all things to himself and restore a suffering world to its original blissful state. At this point, all things will be made new and all tears wiped away.

Humankind was appointed by God to rule over his creation, to care for it and bring the best out of it. (Genesis 1:28) By giving in to evil the first human couple as God's representatives on earth provided a channel through which dark forces could begin to operate within this world. The resultant disharmony and unskilful behaviour caused suffering not only for humankind but all of creation, animate and inanimate. Paul pictures all of creation standing on its tiptoes waiting for its release from suffering. (Romans 8:18-23) And so, the Tree of Life points to God, Father, Son and Holy Spirit, re-creating the world and liberating it from suffering.

We may locate this period that we are now living in as lying between the Tree of Shame and the Tree of Life. As followers of Jesus we participate in his reconciling of all things to their original purpose, and this involves us in reaching out to those who do not yet follow Christ, as well as opposing godless behaviour and structures. (Colossians 1:19) Paul talks about having received the ministry and message of reconciliation; indeed, he uses the image of being an ambassador of Christ. (2 Corinthians 5:17-20) Geoff Grogan (2007:50) explains how, in Paul's time, a Roman military commander would, after defeating his enemies, send his ambassador to inform them of the terms of peace. Rather than the conquering people, we may think here of the conquering of the evil powers who, by various means, control the people. In this passage, Paul describes how he implores people to be reconciled to God; Grogan points out the humble nature of Paul's engagement with those he speaks to. There is a mismatch between the status and rhetoric of an ambassador and Paul's beseeching and continuous pleading. Yet God, who dispatched Paul on this ministry of reconciliation, deeply cares for the people He has sent him to, and Paul cares for them as well. This 'pleading and imploring' ministry calls those who reach out to the Buddhist world to the hard work of learning a religious framework, investing in relationships on a no-strings attached basis and, most probably, learning a language as well.

Conclusion

The Kingdom of God has certain distinctive features, and different images are utilized to highlight these features.[6] Jesus told many stories to illustrate the multi-faceted nature of the Kingdom of God. For example, the value of the kingdom is expressed by the story of the pearl merchant who sells all his pearls in order to own a very valuable one. The comparison of the Kingdom of God to yeast points to the capacity of the kingdom to grow organically and in an imperceptive manner. Interestingly, I have not heard anyone complain about the number and variety of these stories; yet when we come to defining the nature and theological implications of the death of Christ, many people argue for a single explanation or understanding. But why can we not have two, or even more, images which describe the multi-faceted truths of the death and resurrection of Jesus? I find the analogy of *karma* helpful in explaining Jesus suffering the punishment of our sins and giving us his righteousness. However, I think it is worth investigating the cosmic victory of Christ over Satan secured on the Tree of Shame, and the implications of that for the deliverance from dark forces as well as their ultimate

---

[6] There is a useful article on the Kingdom of God by H Ridderbos, 1962 'Kingdom of God: Kingdom of Heaven' in J Douglas et al (eds) pp. 656-8 *New Bible Dictionary* Leicester: IVP. Ridderbos suggests the Kingdom and the Church could be diagrammed as two concentric circles with Christ at the centre of both. The inner circle represents the Church which is made up of all those who profess faith in Christ the King. The larger circle represents the Kingdom which represents God's redeeming work in Christ throughout the world. The Church shares the Gospel of the Kingdom with the world and, in that sense, points to the Kingdom.

destruction. Just as an ellipse has a major and minor axis, so for me, the cross has two crucial components which need to be emphasized: it deals with the punishment due to us because of our sins, and it entails the defeat of the dark powers who both oppose the advance of the Kingdom of God and oppress humankind.

Pause for reflection

1. In the previous chapter we looked at the substitution theory of the atonement. In this chapter we touched on the *Christus Victor* view which emphasizes the triumph of Christ over all dark forces. Do you have a preference for one of these explanations of the work of Christ, and, if so, why?

Chapter 8

Conclusion

After an examination of the life of Norwegian missionary, Karl Reichelt, we concluded that there were five lessons which we could learn from his ministry to Buddhists.

These are:

1. Keep Christ at the centre of all of life and ministry.

2. Live in missionary encounter with others.

3. Take a contextual approach despite the risks of being misunderstood by others.

4. Study hard to understand the religious world of those we try to reach.

5. Form and sustain genuine friendships.

God

The second chapter examined the life of the Buddha through 12 acts, or 12 significant stages which, allegedly, every Buddha goes through. These 12 acts are a helpful paradigm around which to organise the life of the Buddha. The chapter then went on to set out 12 aspects of Jesus Christ's ministry starting with his eternal existence to his return to our world at some future point.

The third chapter discussed issues such as why the Buddha did not discover God, and if his references to Maitreya, the next Buddha of our world, could be read as a prophecy of Jesus. I suggested that in his teachings about enlightenment, *karma* and the *Dhamma*, the Buddha identified three important aspects of the work of God: the provision of liberation from suffering for those who travel God's path; the bringing about of justice; and the revealing of truth.

In an attempt to discover biblical attitudes to those of other faiths, we examined Paul's response to the plethora of religious images in Athens and how he engaged with different people in the synagogue, market place (*agora*), and the city fathers on Mars Hill. Paul was able to adjust his approach to monotheists, people from primal religious fraternities, those with the latest ideas, and also the gate-keepers of the multi-faceted religious practices of the city of Athens. I also suggested that the prophet Jeremiah was sad and regretful at the presence of idols. Clearly, he longed for the day when people would recognise the emptiness of their inherited religious practice and find in God what they could not find in their gods. Chapter four concludes with a consideration of Abraham who shows deep concern for the people of Sodom. God encouraged Abraham to enter into a conversation with Him. In that conversation with God, Abraham expressed concern for the people of Sodom: indeed, this is arguably the first example of intercessory prayer in the Christian Scriptures.

In chapter four we asked whether it was appropriate to compare God to the *Dhamma*, from both Christian and Buddhist perspectives. I have suggested that we may compare God to the *Dhamma* but that it is a penultimate comparison. This comparison may create a 'space' for Buddhists to reflect on the fact that Jesus claimed he was both Truth (God) and the revealer of Truth (God). A Buddhist thinks that personal existence implies being subject to change and dependence on something else, so whatever else, God cannot be personal. Indeed, that would be a demeaning way to describe him. Through the lens of Hans Küng's four-cornered negation approach, we explored what we mean when we speak of God being personal. The Buddha taught that the existence of an enlightened person in *nibbāna* was beyond our comprehension, yet that should not deter us from trying to attain that state. Buddhists then may pursue the path to an enlightenment which they do not yet understand because they believe that it is both possible and worth reaching. In a similar way, God is both the one that is being sought and the one who makes it possible for him to be found.

Self

Chapter five considered the Buddhist understanding of the Five Bundles, or aggregates of sentient existence. We looked at the Buddha's encounter with Saccaka and Nāgasena's conversation with King Milinda. We examines a number of Buddhist understandings of self, in particular the Madhyamaka, Yogācāra, Zen and Puggalavādin traditions. While we came across some complexities, we can conclude that the Buddha was simply trying to help people eliminate self-interest and respond appropriately to the changes of life and the anxiety that such changes can generate. Eliminating self-interest, he taught, would lead away from the suffering caused by attachment. We discussed Christian understandings of self and the tension Christians experience in genuine self-effort and relying on God's power. And, while we do make rigorous effort, can it really be considered *self*-effort when it is God who empowers us?

Salvation

The penultimate chapter uses the idea of *karma*, the concept of a 'go-between person', and the possibility of the transfer of merit to explain what Christ achieved through his death and resurrection and the relevance of that for humankind. We explored possible Buddhist reactions to this 'redemptive analogy.'

The final chapter draws from the Christus Victor understanding of the death and resurrection of Jesus Christ. Here Christ is viewed as a triumphant warrior who, on the Tree of Shame (1 Peter 2:14) defeats the devil and all dark forces, and makes it possible for all who wish to be released from the powers of darkness. The chapter, indeed the book, concludes with the amazing picture of the Tree of Life. (Revelation 22:1-5) This flags up the return of the cosmic conqueror to our world and the final step in the total defeat of evil and the reconciliation and restoration of everything to its original purpose. We live between the Tree on which Christ bore our sins (1 Peter 2:24) and the Tree of Life. (Revelation 22:2) And together, we partner with Jesus Christ in his reconciling of all things to himself. (Colossians 1:20) If we view our lives through this lens, then even our routine activities can be transformed into an exciting adventure.

On this journey, I am constantly reminded of two challenging truths. The first is from Karl Barth: 'If we pray then God will act in a different way than if we don't pray.' The second is a paraphrase of words which I heard from a missionary reflecting on decades of service: 'If Christ's love is in our hearts, then the people we are called to will be in our hearts. If they are in our hearts, then we will be in their hearts.'

Enjoy the adventure of reaching out to the Buddhist world!

Paths To Enlightenment In Theravāda And Mahāyāna Buddhism

This appendix examines the paths to enlightenment in Theravāda, the southern tradition of Buddhism, and Mahāyāna, the eastern tradition of Buddhism. Mahāyāna includes a considerable number of Buddhist fraternities, including Zen, Pure Land and Nicheren. This is a brief overview, so we will only cover the fundamentals of the bodhisattva path, as well as an explanation of enlightenment in the Zen tradition.

We begin, however, with some comments on the emergence of the Theravāda and Mahāyāna schools of Buddhism.

The Theravāda Tradition

Theravāda Buddhism is found largely in Sri Lanka, Myanmar, Thailand, Laos and Cambodia. The Theravāda traditions were brought to the West by the SE Asian diaspora and the missionary monks who later went to establish and support these communities. Theravādins believe that the Pali canon preserves the original teachings of the Buddha. They also view the Buddha as a human figure who, drawing on the wisdom of countless previous lives, achieved enlightenment by himself. In contrast, the Mahāyāna tradition sees the Buddha more of a divine being who projected himself into our world to show the path away from suffering to enlightenment.

It appears that some difference emerged between two groups of monks in the early *saṅgha*, most likely at the Buddhist Second Council, which took place at Viasali some 100 years after the passing away[1] of the Buddha. The conflict was between those who wished for additional monastic regulations and those who saw no need for change. The desire to tighten up on monastic practice may have arisen from wanting to maintain high standards for those being ordained into the *saṅgha*. The reformers were referred to as the Sthaviravāda. (Sanskrit; Pali, Vibhajjavāda or Theravāda.) Theravāda means 'those who adhere to the teachings of the elders'. The group who did not wish to add further restrictions to the code of monastic discipline (*vinaya*) referred to themselves as the Mahāsāṅghika, 'those who belong to the universal *saṅgha*'. (Harvey, 1990:75)

> By the eleventh century CE, what is today designated as the Theravāda became the dominant form of Buddhism in Sri Lanka, achieving a similar status in Burma in the same century, and in Cambodia, Thailand, and Laos by the thirteenth and fourteenth centuries. (Buswell and Lopez, 2013:904)

[1] The Buddha's final entry into *nibbāna* is referred to as *parinibbāna*.

The Emergence of Mahāyāna

Broadly speaking, the Mahāyāna movement had its origins in the group which identified itself as the Mahāsāṅghika. Its main distinction is a commitment to certain Scriptures which it considers to be the words of the Buddha. These Scriptures set out the path to achieving buddhahood by following the bodhisattva path. This approach differed from the Theravāda path, which focuses on a four stage approach resulting in arahatship[2] or enlightenment. Mahāyāna also developed a new cosmology arising from meditative practices, which portrayed the Buddha as a glorified, transcendent being. It may have been that the *Bhakti* (devotional) tradition in Hinduism gave some Buddhists the notion for compassionate deities who could be entreated for help.

Until fairly recently, Mahāyāna was considered to be a lay protest against monastic dominated Buddhism, which was excessively scholarly. Current scholarly thinking, however, understands that Mahāyāna did not emerge as a well-defined fraternity. Gethin (1998:4-5) comments:

> [F]ar from being a popular lay movement, it seems increasingly likely that it began as a minority monastic movement and remained such for several hundred years, down to at least the fifth century CE. Moreover, what is becoming clearer is that many elements of Buddhist thought and

---

[2] Someone who has followed the path of Buddhism to full enlightenment is referred to in the Theravāda tradition by the Pali term *arahat* or *arahant*. When discussing this concept in the Mahāyāna tradition, the Sanskrit word *arhat* is used.

practice that were once thought to be characteristics of the emerging Mahāyāna were simply developments within what has been called by some 'mainstream' Buddhism.

Mahāyāna, however, did not reject the earlier form of Buddhism from which it emerged; rather it viewed it as having a more basic understanding of the Buddha's teaching. The term Mahāyāna often appears in contrast to Hīnayāna or the 'Lesser Vehicle'. Hīnayāna was a term used to refer to those who did not accept the Mahāyāna *sutras* as the word of the Buddha. Mahāyāna means the 'Greater Vehicle,' perhaps conveying the idea that more people would want to travel on the Mahāyāna 'raft', as that tradition offered a more appealing practice. There are many spiritual beings to assist the Mahāyāna aspirant towards enlightenment, and possibilities to engage in useful service to those trapped in ignorance and suffering. This is in contrast to the relatively solitary nature of the path of the Theravāda Buddhist. Buswell and Lopez (2013:904) remind us that 'in the 1950's the World Fellowship of Buddhists adopted a formal resolution replacing the pejorative term Hīnayāna with the designation Theravāda in description of the non-Mahāyāna tradition'.

Different fraternities emerged within Mahāyāna tradition and, in time, it included philosophical schools such as Madhyamika and Yogācāra—which we touched on in our study of 'self' in chapter 5. In addition to Mahāyāna, the Vajrayāna ('Diamond or Thunderbolt Vehicle') emerged. This third *yāna* has a strong focus on the esoteric and uses *tantra* for spiritual development thus accelerating the journey towards enlightenment. What we commonly refer to as Tibetan Buddhism has a Mahāyāna orientation, yet it is firmly in the Vajrayāna tradition.

Mahāyāna Buddhism spread from India via the silk route, the same route taken by traders and those going on military expeditions. Many staging points along the route became towns of significant religious importance. Mahāyāna Buddhism spread from India up to China, and then into Korea in the fourth century CE. From Korea, it spread to Japan in the sixth century CE. As it spread, it exercised its capacity to adapt and assimilate rather than confront existing religious practice. A wide variety of fraternities have emerged from Mahāyāna, including Pure Land, Zen and Nichiren.

Stages of Spiritual Development on the Noble Eightfold Path according to Theravāda Buddhism

The Theravāda tradition emphasizes the Eightfold path which, if followed at the higher level, will lead to becoming an *arahat* and attaining enlightenment. We now turn to examine that path which is the middle way between being an ascetic and being indulgent.

The path may be followed at two levels. First, the ordinary or *lokiya* level. Someone on this path is referred to as *puthujjana*, an ordinary person who lacks the qualities of those who operate at the higher level. The ordinary person will do skilful deeds, which will produce good karmic seed. This will result in a pleasant rebirth, one in which there will be the opportunity and ability to develop as a person and acquire merit.

The second level is the transcendent, supramundane, or noble level, *lokuttara*. This path will eventually lead to enlightenment. When one moves from the ordinary to the higher level such a person will be referred to as an *ariya*, a noble person. The transition from rebirth to enlightenment does not come at one moment, but represents progress made over many lives. We now turn to the four stages of that journey within the Theravāda tradition.

The *first stage* is that of the stream-enterer (*sotāpanna*). This is the transition point from the ordinary to the noble level. Such a person enters the stream of the *Dhamma,* and this is the first main step on the stage to full enlightenment. The stream-0enterer has an unwavering confidence in the Triple Gem—the Buddha, the *Dhamma* and the *saṅgha*. Such a person will never be born as a ghost, animal, hell-being (*asura*), and will reach full enlightenment within seven lives.

There are ten fetters holding a person back from enlightenment. The stream-enterer destroys the first three: the delusion of believing in a permanent self; not having a firm commitment to the Triple Gem; and clinging to vows and precepts in an unhealthy, or superstitious way: any form of clinging is unskilful.

The *second stage* is that of the once-returner (*sakadāgāmin*). The person at this stage will be reborn only once more in the realm of sense-desire, either as a human or a god. The once-returner almost destroys two additional fetters to the stream-enterer, which are the desire for sensual gratification, and feelings of ill will or hatred. These two fetters are not quite destroyed, as there are subtle traces remaining.

The *third stage* is that of the non-returner (*anāgāmin*). This is one who does not have the insight to be fully enlightened. When such a person dies he will be reborn in the first of the five 'pure abodes' where only non-returners are born. In that heaven he will mature his insight until he becomes fully enlightened, as an *arahat* god. The non-returner fully destroys the fourth fetter of desire for sense gratification, which is why he will not be reborn into a sense-world. The fifth fetter of ill will or hatred is also fully destroyed.

The *fourth stage* on the Path followed at the higher level is the fully enlightened being or *arahat*. At this point, the person enters into a state of enlightenment as the fires of greed, hatred and delusion have been extinguished. This state is called 'enlightenment with substrate', or 'remainder'. The bundles of firewood are still there, but they are not on fire because the fires have been extinguished and so the *arahat* is cool! The *arahat* still experiences suffering, as a result of reaping the rewards of past karmic fruit. There is however, no mental pain as the *arahat* does not identify pain as 'his'. He has the insight to see perfectly into absolute truth, the ultimate, and he knows that 'me' and 'mine' are conventional truths. There is no concept of 'I'; that is an illusion. The *arahat* sees himself simply as a set of changing phenomena. The *arahat* then has destroyed the remaining five fetters. These are: attachment to physical goods; attachment to non physical conditions or states, include the attachment to power, status or reputation; lingering forms of conceit; restlessness or rushing about—the opposite to calmness, a great quality in Buddhism; and spiritual ignorance.

Three key differences between Mahāyāna and Theravāda Thinking

Let us remind ourselves of three important points. First, the Māhāyanist sees a huge difference in power and knowledge between the *arhat* and a Buddha. For a Māhāyanist, the Buddha is less of a historical figure and more of a transcendental being who appears as a transformation body—appearing as a man for the purpose of teaching. The difference in power and knowledge between the Historical Buddha and the *arhat* is much less in the Theravāda tradition. In effect, the Mahāyāna Buddhist would say arhatship is such a tiny step on the scale of enlightenment that it is simply not worth aiming for.

Second, the *arhat* is understood by those in the Mahāyāna tradition as being rather selfish, concerned only for their own release from suffering. The Mahāyāna Buddhist sees the *arhat* as lacking the great compassion (*mahākaruṇa*) of the bodhisattva. True, there is a concept of the *bodhisattva* in Theravāda Buddhism, but it is very much for the heroic minority. The Theravāda tradition says that the *arahat* 'has done all he has to do, there is nothing left to do'; this is viewed by the Mahāyanist as lacking in compassion, and at this point they ask 'What about the billions who are suffering on earth and in other abodes?' The *bodhisattva* then is focused on the achievement of *universal* enlightenment, not merely the achieving of *individual* enlightenment, but the liberation of all sentient beings. The body that the *bodhisattva* is in is not their own, but belongs to *all* beings. Denise Cush (1994:100) writes that 'The infinite compassion of the *bodhisattva* means he or she puts the happiness of all beings in the universe before his or her own, not resting until every being in the universe is saved. In order to accomplish this aim, he or she is willing to suffer anything, even if it means giving up his or her life for others over and over again.' If helping others turns out to involve earning bad *karma*—for instance, in a situation where one might kill a would-be murderer—then the *bodhisattva* is willing to suffer the consequences of hell, if it can help others toward liberation. We may also say that the Mahāyāna path engages much more with the supernatural than the traditional Theravāda path. There is help for the aspirant from heavenly beings and there are relationships with deities and teachers long since departed; this is particularly true in the tantric tradition.

Third, the Theravādin is simply doing what he sees as true according to his understanding of his Scriptures and the tradition handed to him. The *bodhisattva* path is not available. It is already very special that he is following the Eight Fold Path at the higher level rather than the mundane level. The Mahāyāna Buddhist does not delay entering enlightenment, but rather rejects the Theravāda understanding of *nirvāṇa*. The idea of the stream-enterer was, according to the Māhāyanist, simply a basic level of teaching for people without much understanding—a 'skilful means' (*upāya kauśalya*) used by the Historical Buddha to get people started on the path towards enlightenment.

The Ten Stages of the Bodhisattva Path according to Mahāyāna Buddhism

We now examine the Mahāyāna track to enlightenment and eventual buddhahood. There are six main perfections or virtues (*pāramitās*) which are practised in the Mahāyāna tradition in order to reach enlightenment. A further four are usually added to these and these ten correspond to the ten stages of the *bodhisattva* path. At each stage, I will mention the English and Sanskrit names of the stage and also the perfection/virtue on which they focus. These virtues are not practised without reference to the other virtues, but it is deemed appropriate to focus on particular virtues at specific stages on the journey to enlightenment. These virtues which the *bodhisattva* must perfect in order to achieve enlightenment approximate the Eight Fold Path followed by the Theravādin Buddhist who wishes to achieve enlightenment.

Stage One: Joyful (*pramuditā*). The perfection is giving (*dāna*). This stage is so named because there is a 'happy confidence of knowing your goal in life'. (Cush, 1994:103) Here the *bodhisattva* focuses on being generous and giving possessions away. The merit gained from this activity will secure buddhahood for himself and others.

Stage Two: Pure (*vimala*). The perfection practised here is morality (*sīla*). The *bodhisattva* urges others to live a moral life, as immoral behaviour leads to unfortunate rebirths. The *bodhisattva*'s meditation becomes developed and they are able to see what normal people are unable to see. For example, the *bodhisattva* can see and pay homage to advanced heavenly beings and Buddhas. Stage Two approximates the stream-enterer of the Theravāda track.

Stage Three: Light Giving (*prabhakari*). The virtue practised here is patience (*kṣānti*). There is a focus on serving others, an activity which develops patience! The mind is purified through meditation and study.

Stage Four: Radiant (*arcismati*). The virtue practised here is vigour (*vīrya*). There is a great deal of energy and vigour at this level, and the *bodhisattva* practises 'all the 37 principles conducive to enlightenment'. (see Cush, 1994:103 for the details) Cush comments that the *bodhisattva* is an example to others and Harvey (1990:123) remarks that this is a good stage for the person to become a monk or nun, as this vocation calls for discipline.

Stage Five: Difficult to conquer (*sudarjaya*). The virtue practiced here is meditation (*dhyāna*). As a consequence the mind is opened up and truths are experienced and understood. As a result, the ability to discern between conventional and absolute truths is exercised. Skills in medicine, science and literature are developed in order to help others. Progress on the path becomes much more rapid, and the *bodhisattva* becomes a teacher of the *Dharma*.

Stage Six: Face-to-face (*abhimukhi*). The virtue practised here is wisdom (*prajñā*). At this stage, the *bodhisattva* moves beyond the Theravāda track to enlightenment and is now on the pathway to supreme buddhahood. Levels one to six are understood to be similar to the Theravāda path which results in becoming an *arhat* but which does not lead to buddhahood. Some say that the *bodhisattva* who reaches this level could enter into personal enlightenment. Yet this would be a violation of the vows made at the beginning of the *bodhisattva* path; the reality is that the Mahāyāna understanding of enlightenment is different to the Theravāda understanding. The Mahāyāna Buddhist understands enlightenment and *saṃsāra* as the two opposite sides of the same spinning coin. Both realities exist in the mind of someone with this level of enlightenment. Certainly at this level distinctions between enlightenment and *saṃsāra*, giver and receiver, and self and other will disappear as the virtue of wisdom is practised. Here Cush (1994:104) remarks that the *bodhisattva* 'does not rest in the enjoyment of this state, but presses on for the salvation of the universe. From this point, he or she is an advanced and holy being.'

Stage Seven: Far Going (*durangama*). The virtue practised here is skilful means (*upāya*). This stage is so called because the *bodhisattva* 'has passed existence as we can imagine it and having gained perfect wisdom can concentrate on *upāya* [skilful means], finding endless ways of helping others to progress spiritually' (Cush, 1994:104). The practitioner may appear in *saṃsāra* in order to assist other sentient beings and is able to assume different forms when appearing to those they wishes to help. Sangharakshita (1987:491) comments that from this point on, all attempts to describe the stages will be a misrepresentation of reality. The progress of the *bodhisattva* is no longer that of an individual, but that of an impersonal cosmic force. 'That we perceive him to be functioning as an individual being is due simply to our mental defilements.'

Stage Eight: Immovable (*acala*). Also referred to as the Stage of Perfection of Vows. The virtue practised here is a focus on the bodhisattva vow (*praṇidhāna*) that was taken by the *bodhisattva* at the beginning of the path to enlightenment. At this level, the *bodhisattva* may transfer merit to those who seek his/her help. Cush (1994:104) comments, 'As a result of perfect wisdom he or she has endless supernatural abilities to use in the task of helping other beings.' The Buddhas remind the *bodhisattva* of their vow and 'once and for all prevent him from relapsing into a personal *nirvāṇa*'. (Sangharakshita, 1987:492)

Stage Nine: Good Intelligence (*sadhumati*). The perfection practised here is power (*bala*). Here, the *bodhisattva* has the ability to relate knowledge and teaching exactly to the needs of sentient beings. This is because they have understood thoughts of others and the way they come to understanding, and have mastered the ability to teach with skilful means. The *bodhisattva* practices the perfection of power and remains in the constant sight of the Buddhas.

Stage Ten: Cloud of the *Dharma* (*Dharmamegha*). The perfection practised here is inner knowledge (*ñāṇa*). At this stage the *bodhisattva* dwells in the Tushita heaven. They have perfect knowledge and are attended to by *bodhisattvas* of the other stages and the buddhas. The Buddhas consecrate this being as a supreme Buddha who has reached the 'endless end' of his path. At this stage, the *bodhisattva* being continuously work for the liberation of all sentient beings. (Sangharakshita, 1987:493)

The Path to Enlightenment in Zen Buddhism

Satori and *kenshō*

The acquiring of a new viewpoint in Zen is referred to as *satori*. It is intuitive rather than intellectual; it is getting the point, or realizing a particular truth. When this 'seeing one's own nature' (*kenshō*) is achieved, then one has 'caught on' (*satori*). The two terms mean the same thing. This 'moment' of 'getting the point' passes away and everything returns to normal but the insight remains. *Kenshō* is not a single experience, but refers to the first glimpse—seeing for the first time. It also refers to other insights, all the way up to the deep insight of full enlightenment. In each experience, the same thing is known but in different degrees of clarity and depth of insight. In the southern school of Zen, Rinzai Zen, *kenshō* experiences are sudden. In Soto Zen, the northern school, there is a more gradual approach to enlightenment brought about by meditation.

DT Suzuki (1870–1966), the well known Buddhist scholar and Zen practitioner, talks about an experience of *kenshō*. He was walking up steps to a building, something he had done thousands of times before, but this time, as he passed the trees, he realized he was the same as the trees yet had not stopped being himself. It was a sudden realization, a *satori*, that there was no 'self' separate from the trees. The *kenshō*, or moment of *satori*, passed but Suzuki retained that moment of non-duality. In Zen style, he could have said 'I am only mind; only mind is everything; everything is nothing. There is only mind and it is the source of its own awakening.'

Cush (1994:145) reflects that it is hard to know that the *satori* claimed by the Zen masters is the same as the enlightenment experience of the Theravādins. Zen practitioners who claim to have experienced *satori* or *kenshō* would not claim to have reached full enlightenment. It may be best to understand these experiences as realizations upon the path. When the experience passes, 'the meditator finds the conventional world is as it was, and yet somehow different: mountains are again mountains, and water is again water'. (Harvey, 1990:275)

Kōan

The Zen master, or *roshi*, will have studied for many years to become qualified to teach Zen. The purpose of the Zen teacher is to enable students to look for truth within themselves. After all, where else will you find truth if nothing exists outside of your mind? The basic assumption of Zen is that there is nothing to teach. The truths of Buddhism are self-evident, and explanation may well obscure the discovery of these truths. Indeed, the teacher may well put obstacles in the path of the student, but when the student fights his way through all of this, the knowledge gained is his own. Mahāyāna stresses that buddha-nature lies within each person and within each sentient being, and the task of the practitioner is to discover and experience it. For this reason, academic study of the texts in Zen is not nearly as important as finding the buddha-nature within. This original mind is pure and is discovered through meditation and through struggling with a series of apparent logic defying statements, called *kōans*.

The practitioner has an experience of touching the buddha nature. The experience passes, but the practitioner is changed by it. The experience, and perhaps subsequent experiences, brings to the practitioner an understanding of the non-duality of all things. In other words, that there are no distinctions between subject and object, the Historical Buddha and you, *nirvāṇa* and *saṃsāra*, training and enlightenment, the teacher and the student. Confusion in complex issues is due to the imprecision of language in explaining concepts. Language relies on opposites to explain a concept: white is the absence of black; in that sense, white cannot be defined without reference to black. These opposites are to be seen as existing in our minds and certainly, *nirvāṇa* and *saṃsāra* exist in the mind of the enlightened person.

Zen meditation focuses on the posture of the body and developing a high state of awareness and, as already mentioned, struggling with a riddle or *kōan*. The *kōan* is an essential feature of the Renzai fraternity of Zen, and is an apparently illogical statement or 'impossible to answer question.' It is used as a meditative technique, possibly in a similar way to the visualisation of a deity in Tantric Buddhism. The *kōan* may function as a discussion point in the interviews between the teacher and the pupil. Once satisfactory answers are received from the pupil, the teacher will give another *kōan* to the student.

The purpose of these enigmatic sayings is to cause people to have an inquiring mind and to challenge their understanding of reality. At a deeper level, the *kōan* helps to create a suitable psychological state in which people may find enlightenment; some would view this as an altered state of consciousness. The *kōan*, then, has the function of short-circuiting a logical linear process.

A practitioner will find no exit from the *kōan*; they feel like they are is locked in a room, running at the wall. In fact, the door is open but to know that requires a turning around and looking at the room in a new way. Some Zen masters talk about the chicken breaking out of the egg. The chick breaks out from the inside by itself, and the teacher's role is as a facilitator, providing help from the outside.

The *kōan* is solved when the student reaches the state of mind which the *kōan* was designed to lead him to, a sense of oneness with the *kōan*. According to the Jesuit priest William Johnston, 'The person who solves the *kōan*s one by one can fairly claim to have imbibed the essentials of Buddhism, to have seen into the essence of things, and be living the life of the Buddha.' (Dumoulin, 1992:127)

The *kōan* is a Chinese invention and carries the typical mark of Chinese spirituality. That is, seeking the deepest levels of meaning in the mundane everyday events of life. While not essential to Zen practice, it is a distinctive feature. There are hundreds of *kōan*s; here are some examples. Which is it that moves, the flag or the wind? The teacher's answer is 'neither, it is the mind that moves'. 'What does Buddha-mind look like?' 'What is your face before your parents' birth?' 'What is the sound of one hand clapping?'

Master Hakuin wrote, regarding the *kōan*: 'It is like a man that is seeking fish. He must first of all look in the water; outside of the water there are no fish. Just so, you who wish to seek Buddha must first of all look into your own mind. Buddha is a product of the mind; outside the mind there is no Buddha.' (Quoted by Blackstone and Josipovic, 1986:79)

Blackstone and Josipovic (1986:76) point out that the three essential qualities which enable one to solve the *kōan* are great faith, great determination, and great doubt. If there is no doubt, then there will be no enquiry. Once the *kōan* practice is completed, the student reflects on the Ten Precepts, which they promised to keep when first entering Zen training. The precepts may now be viewed from an enlightened perspective.

This appears to correspond with stream entry in the Theravāda tradition; the practitioner begins to follow the Noble Eightfold Path at a higher level.

This Appendix has given an overview of the paths to enlightenment in Theravāda and Mahāyāna. These schools represent two different understandings of enlightenment and the spiritual path, and the different goals, in terms of becoming an *arahat* or a high ranking *bodhisattva* and benefactor.

Glossary of Buddhist Terms

aggregate (*khandhas* (P) / *skhandas* (S)) Sometimes referred to as bundles, or components, In the time of the Buddha there was an idea that the five components of body, consciousness, recognition, feelings and mental activities together all constituted 'self'. The Buddha invited people to reflect on 'themselves' and see which of these things they were. Or, were they the sum total of all of these aggregates or components?

akusala An unskilful deed.

anatta No-soul or non-self. One of the three marks of conditioned phenomena. The other two are impermanence (*anicca*) and suffering (*dukkha*)

***arahat* (P) / *arhat* (S)** One who has destroyed all of the 10 fetters which prevents a person achieved enlightenment or *nibbāna* with substrate (aggregates). This is the final stage of the four stages of following the Path at the higher level in the Theravāda tradition.

atta Self.

bhikkhu A mendicant or Buddhist monk.

***bodhisatta* (P) / *bodhisattva* (S)** One who has taken a vow to achieve enlightenment in the process of working for the liberation of all sentient beings. The aim is the enlightenment of all, not simply individual enlightenment.

brahma A class of high gods. The Maha Brahama, chief of the *brahmas* is viewed as a powerful but not fully enlightened being who mistakenly believes himself to have created this world.

Buddha Not a proper name but a title given to one who has achieved enlightenment by himself. In the Theravāda tradition a Buddha is one who has discovered the path that leads to enlightenment but has been lost from the world. Gotama is the present Buddha of this world but, in time, his teachings will be lost to humanity and a new Buddha will emerge whose name is Metteyya (P), Maitreya (S). In the Mahāyāna tradition the attainment of buddhahood comes at the end of a 10 stage process of the bodhisattva path.

dāna Giving, donating, an act of charity.

dependent arising (*paticcasamuppada* (P) / *pratityasamutpada* (S)) The Buddhist doctrine of causality.

deva A god who exists at a lower level to the *brahmas.*

***Dhamma* (P) / *Dharma* (S)** This is not just a Buddhist term; it is an Indian concept with a variety of philosophical and social understandings. *Dhamma* simply is and is not dependent on anyone or anything. It is the Truth of all things. It is also used to describe the teachings of the Buddha.

***dhamma* (P) / *dharma* (S)** mental and physical phenomena; the building blocks that constitute the universe. They are interdependent basic patterns which exist and contribute to the appearance of something or someone. In this sense *dhamma* may be compared to 'quarks' in physics.

dhammarāja A just and righteous king.

dukkha Suffering, the unsatisfactory nature of existence . One of the three marks of conditioned phenomena. The other two are *anatta* (non-self) and *anicca* (impermanence).

Eightfold Path This is the Middle Way that the Buddha taught people to follow. It is a middle way between being an ascetic and being indulgent. The path may be followed at the ordinary (*lokiya*) level. Most Buddhists take this route which focuses on merit making and achieving a good rebirth. The higher (*lokuttara*) level ultimately leads to enlightenment (*nibbāna*) and begins when the practitioner achieves stream entry (plunging into the stream of the *Dhamma*); this is the first of the four stages of enlightenment. (Please see the appendix for further details.) The Eightfold Path has eight factors. The first two have to do with wisdom (*paññā*), they are right understanding and right thought. The next three have to do with moral virtue (*sīla*), they are right speech, right action and right livelihood. The final two factors are concerned with taking a meditative approach (*samādhi*), and are right mindfulness and right concentration. These aspects of the path could be considered as training opportunities for our development rather than rules which need to be kept.

eon This is an incalculable unit of time. Traditionally, it is considered to be the time it would take to wear down a seven mile high granite mountain by rubbing it with a piece of fine cloth once every century!

***kamma* (P) /*karma* (S)** The intentional good and bad actions whose pleasant and unpleasant results are experienced later in life and subsequent lives.

karuṇā 'compassion.' This is one of four 'immeasurable' qualities. The other three are: *mettā* (lovingkindness), *mudita* (rejoicing in the joy of others) and *upekkhā* (equanimity).

kilesa 'Mental defilements'. The standard list of 10 is: greed, hatred, delusion, conceit, speculative views, sceptical doubt, mental topor, restlessness, shamelessness and lack of moral dread or fear.

kusala Skilful action.

lokiya Worldly or pertaining to this world.

lokuttara Pertaining to a higher world, or supramundane.

Four Noble Truths (*ariya-sacca*) These truths follow the pattern of: diagnose the disease, discover its cause, determine whether the illness is curable and if so, prescribe a cure. The truths are: i) suffering is our illness ii) the cause is our craving and clinging iii) the cure is to get rid of our craving and clinging, and iv) the way to health (enlightenment) is to follow the Middle Way or Eightfold Path.

Madhyamaka One of the two main schools of Mahāyāna, the other being Yogācāra.

Mahāyāna Literally meaning the 'great vehicle' or 'raft'. Sometimes referred to as Eastern Buddhism, a very broad movement of Buddhist schools out with the Theravāda and Tibetan (Vajrayāna) schools of Buddhism.

mantra A word or phrase which has spiritual significance for the user. For example, the reciting of the *mantra* may sow good karmic seed, release power within the user, or bring tranquillity.

maṇḍala A sacred circle representing a sacred realm. It often consists of concentric circles, enclosed by a square.

Māra A tempter figure who tries to entrap others. It is sometimes a term used to refer to death or a symbol of that which holds a person back from gaining enlightenment.

ñāṇa Inner-knowledge.

non-returner (*anāgāmin*) One who has attained the third of the four stages on the path to enlightenment. When such a person passes away s/he will be reborn in the first of the 'five pure abodes' where only non-returners are born. The non-returner destroys the fourth fetter of desire for gratification of the senses – which is why s/he is not reborn into a sense-world.

nibbāna **(P)** / *nirvāṇa* **(S)** the extinguishing of the fires of greed, hatred and delusion. That which is unconditioned and lies beyond *saṃsāra*.

once returner (*sakadāgāmin*) A being who has achieved the second stage of following the Eightfold Path at the higher level. A person at this stage will be reborn only once more in the realm of sense-desire i.e. a human or god.

paññā Wisdom.

parinibbāna The final entering of a Buddha into *nibbāna*. The Buddha entered into *nibbāna* with substrate (i.e. with the Five Aggregates) at his enlightenment at the age of 35. At his death (*parininibbāna*) at the age of 80, the Buddha entered a state of *nibbāna* without substrate (without the Five Aggregates).

peta A ghost-like being who returns to the human realm due to strong attachments to it. This is the very worst possible form of rebirth.

samādhi A state of concentration.

samatha A model of meditation where the meditator achieves a level of bliss and calm.

saṃsāra All states out with *nibbāna*. A word used to describe the 'wanderings on' of rebirths. That said, no distinction is made between *saṃsāra* and *nibbāna* in the Mahāyāna tradition as both define each other. In the mind of the enlightened person *saṃsāra* and *nibbāna* co-exist.

saṅgha The Buddhist order of monks (and in some traditions nuns). Some traditions understand the *saṅgha* to also include lay Buddhists.

santi Peace.

sīla Ethics or good moral conduct.

stream enterer (*sotāpanna*) This is the first stage (in the Theravāda tradition) on the road to attaining full enlightenment. This is the transition point from following the Eightfold Path at the ordinary to the higher level.

***suññatā* (P) / *śunyatā* (S)** Emptiness, the ultimate way things are.

tantra Rituals or Scriptures associated to esoteric practice (often representing a faster but more dangerous track to enlightenment) within certain Buddhist schools e.g. Vajrayāna Buddhism

Theravāda This tradition of Buddhism is found largely in Sri Lanka, Myanmar, Thailand, Laos and Cambodia. It is sometimes referred to as Southern Buddhism. In the past the somewhat disrespectful term Hīnayāna or 'small vehicle' was used to describe the tradition. Theravadins believes that the Pali canon preserves the original teachings of the Buddha. They also view the Buddha as a human figure who, drawing on the wisdom of countless previous lives achieved enlightenment by himself. In contrast, the Mahāyāna tradition sees the Buddha more of a divine being who projected himself into our world to show the path away from suffering to enlightenment.

***Tipiṭaka* (P) / *Tripiṭaka* (S)** The three baskets of the Buddhist Scriptures. The Scriptures were first written on palm leaves and then arranged into one of three baskets – *Vinaya* (monastic discipline), *Suttas* (P) / *Sūtras* (S) (the teachings of the Buddha or his disciples), and the *Abhidhamma* (further teachings).

Upanishads A set of sacred brahamanical texts included in the *Veda*.

Veda The corpus of sacred brahmanical texts.

Vinaya Discipline for Buddhist monks (and nuns) and one of the three divisions (baskets) of the Buddhist Scriptures.

vipassanā A form of meditation which focuses on insight into reality.

Yogācāra One of two main schools of Mahāyāna Buddhism; the other being Madhyamaka.

Bibliography

Archer, D., C. Puntis, and T. Watkins (2001). *What Does the Bible Say About The Matrix Trilogy?* Southampton: Damaris Trust.

Aulen, G. *Christus Victor.* Ed. by A. Herbert. London: SPCK.

Barth, K. (1964). *Prayer and Preaching.* London: SCM.

Bauckham, R. (1995). *The Theology of Jürgen Moltmann.* Edinburgh: T and T Clark.

Beasley-Murray, GR (1999). *John.* Vol. 36. Word Biblical Commentary. Nashville, TN: Thomas Nelson.

Berkhof, L. (1971). *Systematic Theology.* London: The Banner of Truth Trust.

Blackstone, J and Z Josipovic (1986). *Zen for Beginners.* New York: Writers' and Readers' Publishing.

Bonhoeffer, D (1959). *The Cost of Discipleship.* London: SCM Press.

Boon-Itt, B. (2007). "The Goal of Life: Nibbana and the Kingdom of God- A Study of the Dialogue between Christianity and Theravada Buddhism in Thailand as represented by Buddhist and Christian Writings from Thailand in the Period

1950-2000". PhD thesis. Open University and St John's College Nottingham.

Bowers, J. S. (1996). *Dhammakaya Meditation in Thai Society*. Bangkok: Chulalongkorn University Press.

Boyd, G. (2006). "Penal Substitution View". In: *The Nature of the Atonement*. Ed. by J Beilby and P Eddy. Downers Grove, Illinois: IVP Academic, pp. 23–53.

Boyd, J. W. (1975). *Satan and Mara—Christian and Buddhist Symbols of Evil*. Leiden: Brill.

Brinkman, M.E (2009). *The Non-Western Jesus: Jesus as Bodhisattva, Avatara, Guru*. en. London: Routledge.

Bruce, F.F. (1988). *The Book of the Acts*. Grand Rapids, Michigan: William B Eerdmans Publishing Company.

Buddha Dharma Education Association (2012). *The Five Aggregates*. http://www.buddhanet.net/funbud14.htm.

Buddhadasa (1967). *Christianity and Buddhism*. en. Sinclaire Thomson Memorial Lecture, Fifth series. Bangkok: Sublime Life Mission Keesarn Publishers.

— (1969). *Dhamma: The World Saviour*. en. Bangkok: Mahamakutrajavididyalaya.

Burns, C (2003). "Soul-Less Christianity and the Buddhist Empirical Self: Buddhist – Christian Convergence". In: *Buddhist – Christian Studies* 23, pp. 87–100.

Buswell Jr, Robert E and Donald S Lopez Jr (2013). *The Princeton Dictionary of Buddhism*. Princeton, NJ: Princeton University Press.

Cabezón, J.I. (2000). "A God but Not a Savior". In: *Buddhists Talk about Jesus: Christians Talk about the Buddha*. Ed. by

T.C. Muck and R.M. Gloss. New York: Continuum, pp. 17-31.

Callaway, T. (1976). *Zen Way Jesus Way*. Tokyo: Charles E Tuttle Co.

Calvin, J. (1959). *Calvin's New Testament Commentaries: John 11-21 and First John*. Ed. by T Torrance and D. Torrance. Trans. by T. Parker. Grand Rapids, Michigan: Eerdmans.

— (1961). *The Gospel According to Saint John*. en. Edinburgh: Oliphants.

— (1992). *Genesis*. en. Ed. by John King. Edinburgh: The Banner of Truth Trust.

Carus, P., ed. (1994a). *The Gospel of Buddha*. Oxford: Oneworld.

— ed. (1994b). *The Gospel of Buddha*. Oneworld.

Chanthavongsouk, L. (1999). *Buddha's Prophecy of the Messiah*. en. La Mirada, California: The Lao Conference of Churches.

Cioccolanti, S. (2007). "From Buddha to Jesus: An Insider's View of Buddhism and Christianity". en. In: *Sweet Life International*.

Collinson, S. (2004). *Making Disciples*. en. Carlisle: Paternoster Press.

Coomaraswamy, A. (1916). *Buddha and the Gospel of Buddhism*. New York: GP Putnam's Sons.

Cush, D. (1994). *Buddhism*. en. A Student's Approach to World Religions. London: Hodder and Stoughton.

Davis, John R (1998). *Poles Apart?: Contextualizing the Gospel in Asia*. Bangalore, India: Theological Book Trust.

Dumoulin, Heinrich (1992). *Zen Buddhism in the Twentieth Century*. New York and Tokyo: Weatherhill.

Eilert, Hakan (1974). *Boundlessness: Studies in Karl Ludvig Reichelt's Missionary Thinking with Special Regard to the Buddhist Christian Encounter*. en. Arhus: Forlaget Arcs.

Evans, C. A. (2001). *Mark 8:27 to 12:20*. Nashville, TN: Thomas Nelson Publishers.

— (2001-03). *Mark 8:27 to 12:20*. Nashville: Thomas Nelson Publishers.

Fung, R. (1988). *The Epistle to the Galatians*. en. Grand Rapids, Michigan: William B Eerdmans Publishing Company.

Gethin, R. (1998). *The Foundations of Buddhism*. en. Oxford: Oxford University Press.

Gluer, W. (1968). "The Encounter between Christianity and Chinese Buddhism during the Nineteenth Century and the First Half of the Twentieth Century". en. In: *Ching Feng* 11.3, pp. 39–57.

Gombrich, R. (1988). *Theravada Buddhism*. en. London: Routledge.

Grenz, S. (2000). *Theology for the Community of God*. Grand Rapids, Michigan: W.B. Eerdmans.

Grimm, G. (1994). *The Doctrine of the Buddha*. Delhi: Mortilal Banarsidass Publishers Private Limited.

Grogan, G. (2007). *2 Corinthians*. en. Fearn, Ross-shire: Christian Focus.

Grudem, W. (1994). *Systematic Theology*. Leicester: IVP.

Haas, M., ed. (1964). *Thai-English Student's Dictionary*. en. Stanford: Stanford University Press.

Hamilton, S. (1997). "Passionlessness in Buddhism". In: *Scottish Journal of Religious Studies* 18.1, pp. 3–23.

Harris, E. (2005). "Human Existence in Buddhism and Christianity— A Christian Perspective". en. In: *Buddhism and Christianity in Dialogue: The Gerald Weisfeld Lectures 2004*. Ed. by P. Schmidt-Leukel. Norwich: SCM Press, pp. 29–52.

Harvey, P. (1990). *An Introduction to Buddhism*. Cambridge: Cambridge University Press.

— (1995). *The Selfless Mind: Personality, Consciousness and Nirvana in Early Buddhism*. Richmond: Curzon Press.

— ed. (2001). *Buddhism*. London: Continuum.

Hawthorne, G. (1983). *Philippians*. Vol. 43. Word Bible Commentary. Waco: Word Books.

Henry, M. (1995). *Matthew Henry's New Testament Commentary*. Ed. by David Winter. London: Hodder and Stoughton.

Hunt, G. (2010). *New Buddha Way: Insight*. Vol. 3. Buddha Dharma Series. Godalming: Laleston Press.

Inagaki, Z. (2000). *Amida the Infinite: An Introduction to Shin Buddhism*. en. Woodville, Australia: Horai Association of Australia.

Jackson, P. (1999). "Royal Spirits, Chinese gods, and Magic Monks: Thailand's Boom-Time Religions of Prosperity". In: *South East Asia Research* 7.3, pp. 245–320.

Jensen, I. (1969). *Life of Christ: A Self-Study Guide*. en. Chicago: The Moody Bible Institute of Chicago.

Keenan, J. P. (1995). *The Gospel of Mark: A Mahayana Reading*. en. Maryknoll, New York: Orbis Books.

Keller, T. (2001). *Real Friendship and the Pleading Priest.* https://www.youtube.com/watch?v=poswQjoLG6I.

Keown, D. (2003). *A Dictionary of Buddhism.* Oxford: OUP.

Kitamori, K. (1965). *Theology of the Pain of God.* Translated from the 1958 Japanese Edition. Richmond, Virginia: John Knox Press.

Knott, K (1998). *Hinduism: A Very Short Introduction.* Oxford: Oxford University Press.

Küng, H. (1993). *Christianity and the World Religions.* London: SCM Press.

Last Days of the Buddha (The Mahā Parinibbana Sutta) (1988). Trans. by Sister Vajira and Story F. Buddhist Publication Society.

Ling, T. (1997). *Buddhism and the Mythology of Evil.* Oxford: Oneworld.

Longenecker, R. (1990). *Galatians.* Word Bible Commentary. Nashville: Thomas Nelson Publishers.

Lorgunpai, S. (1995). "World Lover-World Leaver". Unpublished PhD thesis. New College, University of Edinburgh.

Mackenzie, R (2007). *New Buddhist Movements in Thailand: Towards an Understanding of Wat Phra Dhammakāya and Santi Asoke.* Abingdon: Routledge.

Martin, R. (1974). *Colossians and Philemon.* London: Oliphants.

McArthur, Meher (2004). *Reading Buddhist Art – An Illustrated Guide to Buddhist Signs and Symbols.* London: Thames and Hudson.

Moltmann, J. (1974). *The Crucified God: The Cross of Christ as the Foundation and Criticism of Christian Theology*. London: SCM Press.

Morris, L. (1984). *The Gospel According to John*. Grand Rapids: William B Eerdmans.

Muck, T. (2000). "Missiological Issues in the Encounter with Emerging Buddhism". In: *Missiology* 28.1, pp. 35–46.

Murray, Stuart (1998). *Church Planting*. Milton Keynes: Paternoster Press.

Netland, Harold and Keith Yandell (2009). *Spirituality without God – Buddhist Enlightenment and Christian Salvation*. Milton Keynes: Paternoster Press.

Perkins, J. (1993). *Beyond Charity*. Grand Rapids: Baker Book House.

Petchsongkram, W (1975). *Talk in the Shade of the Bo Tree*. Translated and edited by F.E. Hudgins. Bangkok.

Pierson, P. (2000). "Nestorian Mission". In: *Evangelical Dictionary of World Missions*. Ed. by AS Moreau. Grand Rapids: Baker Books.

Powers, J. (1995). *Introduction to Tibetan Buddhism*. New York: Snow Lion Publications.

Pym, J. (2001). *You Don't Have to Sit on the Floor*. London: Rider.

Rahula, Walpola (1967). *What the Buddha Taught*. London: The Gordon Fraser Gallery Ltd.

Rajavaramuni, Phra (1990). *Thai Buddhism in the Buddhist World*. Bangkok: Mahachulalongkorn University Press.

Reichelt, K. (1937). "Buddhism in China at the present Time and the New Challenge to the Christian Church". In: *The International Review of Missions* 26, pp. 155–166.

— (1938). "The Johannine Approach". In: *The Authority of Faith*. Tambaram Series 1, pp. 90–101.

— (1953). *Meditation and Piety in the Far East*. Ed. by Sverre Holth. Cambridge: James Clarke and Co.

Richardson, D. (1981). "Finding the Eye Opener". In: *Perspectives on the World Christian Movement – A Biblical Reader*. Ed. by R. Winter and S. Hawthorne. Carlisle: Paternoster Press, pp. 67–69.

Ridderbos, H. (1962). "Kingdom of God, Kingdom of Heaven". In: *New Bible Dictionary*. Ed. by J. Douglas. Leicester: IVP, pp. 656–8.

Rienecker, F. and C. Rogers (1980). *Linguistic Key to the New Testament*. Grand Rapids(Michigan): Zondervan Publishing House.

Ross, Andrew (1994). *A Vision Betrayed: The Jesuits in Japan and China 1542 – 1742*. Edinburgh: Edinburgh University Press.

Sangharakshita (1987). *A Survey of Buddhism*. London: Tharpa Publications.

Schreiner, T. (2006). "Penal Substitution View". In: *The Nature of the Atonement*. Ed. by J. Beilby and P. Eddy. Downers Grove, Illinois: IVP Academic, pp. 68–98.

Sharpe, E. (1984). *Karl Ludvig Reichelt: Missionary, Scholar and Pilgrim*. Hong Kong: Tao Fong Shan Ecumenical Centre.

Silva, L. de (1975). *The Problem of the Self in Buddhism and Christianity*. Colombo: The Study Centre for Religion and Society.

Smith, A. (2003). "Missionary Implications of the Key Contrasts between Buddhism and Christianity". In: *Sharing Jesus in the Buddhist World*. Ed. by D. Lim and S. Spaulding. Pasadena, California: William Carey Library, pp. 31-55.

Smith, R. (1984). *Word Bible Commentary: Micah - Malachi*. Waco, Texas: Word Books.

Sorik, A. (1997). "The Cross and the Lotus - The Story of the Christian Mission to Buddhists and KL Reichelt". In: *Areopagus* 9.4, pp. 72-7.

Stanley, B (2012). *Staff Profile*. http://www.ed.ac.uk/schools-departments/divinity/staff-profiles/stanley.

Stott, J. (1968). *The Message of Galatians*. Leicester: IVP.

— (1986). *The Cross of Christ*. Leicester: IVP.

— (1990). *The Message of Acts*. Leicester: IVP.

Strandenoes, T. (2009). "Contextualising the Commitments and Concerns of Dr. Karl Ludvig Reichelt the 21st Century". In: *Swedish Missiological Themes* 97.2, pp. 127-140.

Sunquist, S.W., ed. (2001). *A Dictionary of Asian Christianity*. Cambridge: William B Eerdmans.

Suzuki, D.T. (1957). *Mysticism: Christian and Buddhist*. London: George Allen and Unwin.

Swearer, D.K. (1989). *Me and Mine*. New York: State University of New York Press.

Swearer, D.K (2005). "Buddhadasa". In: *Encyclopaedia of Religion*. Ed. by L. Jones. London: Thomas Gale, pp. 1071-3.

Terwiel, B. (1994). *Monks and Magic*. Bangkok: White Lotus.

Thaiwatcharamas, P. (1983). "God and Christ in the Context of Buddhism". In: *Sharing Jesus in the Two Thirds World*. Ed. by V Samuel and C Sugden. Grand Rapids (Michigan): William B Eerdmans Publishing Company, pp. 204–216.

Thapar, Romila (1986). *A History of India*. Vol. 1. Harmondsworth: Pelican Books.

Thelle, N.R. (1981). "The Legacy of Karl Ludvig Reichelt". In: *International Bulletin of Missionary Research* 5, pp. 65–69.

— (2005). "A Christian Monastery for Buddhist Monks Part II". In: *Ching Feng* 6.2, pp. 131–177.

— (2008). "The Gift of Being Number Two: A "Buzz Aldrin" Perspective on Pioneer Missions". In: *International Bulletin of Missionary Research* 32, pp. 81–4.

Tyra, G. (2013). *A Missional Orthodoxy: Theology and Ministry in a Post-Christian Context*. Downers Grove, Illinois: IVP Academic.

Varasak, Varadhammo (1996). *Suffering and No Suffering*. Hinsdale, Illinois: Buddhadharna Meditation Centre.

Von Stroh, D. (2009). "Buddhadasa, Tamma, Jesus, and the Promise of New Creation". In: *Communicating Christ in Asian Cities*. Ed. by P. De Neui. Pasadena, California: William Carey Library, pp. 225–259.

Ward, K. (1984). *The Living God*. London: SPCK.

Warder, Anthony Kennedy (2000). *Indian Buddhism*. Delhi: Motilal Banarsidass Publ.

Wenham, G. (1994). *Genesis 16-50*. Word Biblical Commentary. Dallas: Word Books.

Williams, P. (2000). *Buddhist Thought: A Complete Introduction to the Indian Tradition.* London: Routledge.

Williamson, G (2014). "In What Ways and to What Extent is God Present to Non-Believers and How Might this Influence our Approach to Faith Sharing?" Unpublished essay for International Christian College. Glasgow.

Winter, B. (1996). "On Introducing Gods to Athens: An Alternative Reading of Acts 17: 18-20". In: *Tyndale Bulletin.* Vol. 47. 1, pp. 71–90.

Wright, C. (2006). *The Mission of God.* Nottingham: IVP.

Wright, N. T. (2008). *Acts for Everyone Part 1 Chapters 1-12.* London: SPCK.

Wuest, K. (1973). *Word Studies in the Greek New Testament.* Vol. 1. Grand Rapids (Michigan): Eerdmans Publishing Co.

Wyatt, D. (1984). *Thailand: A Short History.* New Haven: Yale University Press.

Wyatt, J. (2009). *Matters of Life and Death: Human Dilemmas in the Light of the Christian Faith.* Nottingham: IVP.

Yandell, Keith and Harold Netland (2009). *Buddhism: a Christian exploration and appraisal.* Downers Grove, Illinois: InterVarsity Press.

Young, E. (1972). *The Book of Isaiah.* Grand Rapids, Michigan: Eerdmans Publishing Co.

www.ingramcontent.com/pod-product-compliance
Lightning Source LLC
LaVergne TN
LVHW051358080426
835508LV00022B/2886